DID I MISS ANYTHING?

OTHER BOOKS BY TOM WAYMAN

Poetry:

Waiting For Wayman, 1973
For and Against the Moon: Blues, Yells, and Chuckles, 1974
Money and Rain: Tom Wayman Live!, 1975
Free Time: Industrial Poems, 1977
A Planet Mostly Sea, 1979
Living on the Ground: Tom Wayman Country, 1980
Introducing Tom Wayman, 1980 (USA)
The Nobel Prize Acceptance Speech, 1981
Counting the Hours: City Poems, 1983
The Face of Jack Munro, 1986
In a Small House on the Outskirts of Heaven, 1989

Essays:

Inside Job: Essays on the New Work Writing, 1983
A Country Not Considered: Canada, Culture, Work, 1993

Editor:

Beaton Abbot's Got the Contract, 1974
A Government Job at Last, 1976
Going for Coffee, 1981
East of Main (with Calvin Wharton), 1989
Paperwork, 1991

DID I MISS ANYTHING?

SELECTED POEMS 1973-1993

Tom Wayman

HARBOUR PUBLISHING

Published by
Harbour Publishing Co. Ltd.
P.O. Box 219
Madeira Park, BC Canada V0N 2H0

Printed and bound in Canada
Typeset in Caxton and Kabel DemiBold

Canadian Cataloguing in Publication Data

Wayman, Tom, 1945–
   Did I miss anything? : selected poems, 1973–1993

   ISBN 1-55017-092-9

   I. Title.
PS8595.A943D5 1993   C811'.54   C93-091622-0
PR9199.3.W39D5 1993

ACKNOWLEDGEMENTS

I am grateful to the editors of the periodicals and anthologies in whose pages these poems first appeared. And I deeply appreciate the contribution to my art made by the staffs of the publishing houses who have produced my books: McClelland & Stewart, Macmillan of Canada, Thistledown Press, Turnstone Press, Ontario Review Press, and Harbour Publishing. I would like to particularly acknowledge Howard White of Harbour Publishing. As friend, supporter, colleague and inspiration, as well as publisher, Howie helped create for my poems a feeling of connectedness with a place and people, a sense of belonging, of home.

During most of the years of publication this volume spans, my partner and companion was Perry Louise Millar. Her beneficial impact on my life and work has been incalculable, and she has my loving gratitude for all she has provided of reason, knowledge, soul, heart and humor. I am grateful, too, for the unwavering support of my father, mother and my brother, Mike.

The lives of my friends are woven tightly through my words. A special thank you to my friend Dennis Saleh, who recognizes no boundaries on creativity and the imagination. Each idea he has shared has expanded my sense of the possible.

I wish that each of my dead were still present on this planet in person, so they could receive their copy of this book and respond to it according to their unique selves. But my dead live with me, and thus I give them these poems in the afterlife, with my thanks and affection. Particularly Dennis Wheeler, whose fierce passion for the arts remains a mark against which I measure my shortcomings and achievements.

Finally, I want to acknowledge the children in my life, who are demonstrating an amazing tendency to transform themselves speedily first into teenagers and then adults. Yet they teach me a great deal during this process, as together we shape the future.

Of the new poems here, "Did I Miss Anything?" and "Billy on Industrial Progress" first appeared in *Poetry Northwest*; "Poetry Overdose" first appeared *Triquarterly*, a publication of Northwestern University.

I dedicate this book to everyone who assisted me along the way.

CONTENTS

from FREE TIME: INDUSTRIAL POEMS (1977)

from LIVING ON THE GROUND:
TOM WAYMAN COUNTRY (1980)

Introduction:
GLAD I WAS BORN

This year, 1993, is the twentieth anniversary of the publication of my first book of poems, *Waiting For Wayman*. To mark the occasion, I wanted to make a selection of the best writing I have done to date. Since temporal distance, for me, is a great aid to evaluation and judgment, *Did I Miss Anything?* offers the most memorable poems from my first six books, which appeared between 1973 and 1983. Also here are a sampling from my two most recent collections (from 1986 and 1989), which remain in print from Harbour Publishing, and some new poems that bring the reader up to the present.

These two decades have been a wonderful experience for me as a writer, and for my poems. Together we have had more than our share of recognition, media attention, public readings and literary festivals, magazine and anthology publication, grants, translations into other languages, awards, writer-in-residenceships . . . everything, in fact, that any author could want. Meanwhile, I have watched helplessly as the art form I love has diminished in the public's perception of its value and importance. Arrayed against poetry are a swelling and seemingly unbeatable coalition that includes a declining readership for any written material, the adoption of poetry as an instrument of torture in our secondary school classrooms, and the confusion by a number of authors between obscurity of presentation and depth of thought, and between exclusiveness and superiority.

However, like a steadily-promoted deck officer on the *Titanic*, I have been having a marvellous time as a writer. During the past twenty years my poems have taken me to fascinating places, and introduced me to many astonishing and delightful people, that otherwise I never would have known. I also have been privileged to help bring into being—along with dozens of others—a new movement in poetry, literature, and the arts generally: the incorporation into the human story of the actual conditions and effects of daily employment. In this task my contribution has been the editing of anthologies and the writing of essays, in addition to my own poems. The endeavor, however, has introduced me and my poetry to non-literary audiences that the already-blazed cultural trails would never have led me to. These audiences, along with the first-year college classes I teach, have provided me with a continual reminder of the ever-widening gap between literary pursuits and the concerns of a majority of my fellow citizens.

And yet, throughout twenty years my poetic aim has been to provide an accurate depiction of our common everyday life. I have tried to combine this with a sense of humor and with a vision of a better possibility for people than what we have so far achieved. My hope is that the latter two aspects of my writing provide perspective on the balance of what I portray. As for spirituality, I long ago was a convert to the concept expressed by Robert Bly in his poem "Turning Away From Lies" (from *The Light Around the Body*, 1967): "The Kingdom of Heaven does not mean the next life / . . . The two worlds are both in this world."

Overall, my intention is that the complexities revealed by my poems should be the complications of our everyday existence, rather than newly-created difficulties or mysteries generated by tricks of language or poetic form. Clarity, honesty, accuracy of statement have been my goals—subject to, naturally, the limits of human discourse found in *every* genre or means of communication. My aim is that my poems should be useful: to myself, and to others who share my community and world. I mean these poems to be a gift; I want my poetry to be a tender, humorous, enraged, piercing, but always accurate depiction of where we are—as individuals functioning in a society, and as members of a rawly self-conscious species now occupying the third planet from a nondescript star.

Much that I have encountered in my life in the way of events, individuals, and popular and high art has influenced my writing. In poetry, two important Canadian influences were Earle Birney and Al Purdy. I was impressed by the range of their subject matter and by their careful craftsmanship, even though the latter often appears within a deceptively conversational tone. Internationally, my major influences were T.S. Eliot and Pablo Neruda. I attended university in a period when

Eliot dominated English letters. For many years the shadow of Eliot lay across whatever I wrote; my "Asphalt Hours, Asphalt Air" is an attempt to banish that dry darkness forever. The poem is based closely on Eliot's "The Waste Land," but my poem places its concerns within a landscape of contemporary North American industrial and societal myths and activities. Neruda has been a much sunnier and more vigorous model for me. The Chilean poet's attention to the real elements of this world—things—finds reflection in my writing in "Kitchen Poem," for example. And Neruda's huge affection for people has influenced many poems of mine, including "New and Used," where the initial inspiration came from Neruda's poem about a Valparaiso clockmaker.

What I bring to poetry that these writers do not is the centrality of daily work to our life. I believe that to try to articulate the human story without depicting the core of daily existence is a tragic mistake. We all dream of a world without work, but we remain victims of our form of social organization as long as we—and our art—refuse to honestly consider how our jobs shape us, positively and negatively.

An imaginary world where we do not work to survive may be an adolescent dream, and may offer a picture of a more beautiful existence than is now an actual possibility for us. But sooner or later a functioning adult must face and make choices that involve work. The alternative is to remain dependent—on luck, chance, friends, relatives, the mercy of those with more power, the state. That is why I believe what I write is the literature of the future: an adult literature. As I stated in my 1983 book of essays, *Inside Job*:

> Just as a child or adolescent often does not under-
> stand work or money, so our literature mostly has
> ignored these and focussed instead on the unlikely
> lives of those whose day-to-day existence apparently
> is not governed by concerns of work or money: the
> rich, killers, outlaws, or fantastic representations of
> people doing certain real jobs (doctors, cowboys,
> policemen, and so on).
>
> The new work writing takes up the challenge of
> portraying the world an adult sees and attempts to
> understand and/or change. A grown person who

constantly evades having to cope with reality, who lives in a world of dreams however beautiful, we consider immature if not mentally ill. The contemporary industrial writing provides maturity and a healthy balance to literature.

Because most of us do not like what we see when we look at our jobs, we frequently engage as individuals and a community in acts of denial about daily employment. Most jobs constitute a "distinct society" we participate in each day, where during the central part of our existence most of the democratic rights and privileges Canadians enjoy off the job are suspended. Briefly, we live our productive lives—the majority of our waking hours—as free-lance serfs. We are free to choose and change the masters we will obey for money, free to be destitute or marginal, free to go into debt, free to purchase as many of life's necessities and/or drugs and toys as our rate of remuneration permits. We are even free to employ other serfs. But most of us at work have no significant control over what happens to us, over who gives us orders, over the organization of production, over the distribution of the wealth our labor produces, over the social uses of what we create. The alternative of self-employment often turns into self-exploitation as we strive to remain competitive with enterprises employing serfs.

Our denial of this state of unfreedom leads ourselves and many of our cultural products to ignore the realities of the present, as well as the painful and frightening and exhilarating effort necessary to change the present. Instead, there is an urge to leap forward to an imaginary era where what is denied today never has to be looked at or understood, or changed for the better in the face of enormous opposition. But an adult literature does not pretend to have already resolved our current dilemmas; this literature cannot be categorized as post-modern, post-industrial, post-feminist, etc. Adult art recognizes itself instead as pre-liberation. Firmly anchored in the realities of the modern era, such art acknowledges and responds to the industrial organization of the globe and that organization's attendant inequalities and injustices concerning class, gender, race, ecosystems and more.

This is not to say that an adult poetry must be dreary. No

one has ever, for example, accused my writing of that. To an adolescent, adulthood may seem a reduced state of being, as responsibilities and commitments limit the boundless possiblities of dream. But to a functioning adult, skills and knowledge gained make possible the creation of a life, not merely the response to it. This sense of strength, of efficacy, of potential power to solve problems that are encountered and thus to tangibly shape the world a better way, move the competent adult out of passiveness into life-enhancing activities that can benefit both the self and the surrounding community.

In any case, every human emotion is part of adult life, that is, of work. Joy, wonder, laughter, games, rebellion, lust, love can be experienced at the jobsite, since work—however undemocratically structured today—is in its last analysis a place where human beings gather to remanufacture the world. Yet every activity found in the shop or office or factory is warped by its occurrence within a more-or-less authoritarian environment, just as our lives are warped by our and our neighbors' daily participation in this environment. We deny this, as a society, at our peril. I do not see my role as a literary artist as contributing—through denial—to the ongoing affliction of myself or my friends and co-workers.

Instead, the task of helping build an adult literature remains an immense challenge, that I know will involve my writing for many years ahead. The two decades represented by this book sketched the outline of my participation in a new and maturer direction for poetry. I cannot imagine a more exciting time to practice one's writing than at the beginnings of so momentous a shift in art.

As an author, I owe much to many people who have helped me and my poems; some of these are listed on the Acknowledgements page here. But the core of my gratitude must go to my readers, who despite the prevailing aesthetic have welcomed not only my poems but also the vision of literature toward which I struggle. It is ultimately my readers' response that has made my artistic adventures during these decades such intensely rewarding ones. How can I express an overwhelming gratitude? Near the end of Marcel Camus' 1958 film *Orfeu Negro* (*Black Orpheus*), the grieving Orpheus asks this same question of his beloved Euridice, whose dead body he is carrying in his arms. She has given him total happiness, has immeasurably enriched his life; how can he tell her this? His friend Hermes, who like Orpheus in Camus' version of the myth is a Rio de Janeiro transit company employee, advises: "Say a poor man's word, Orpheus: 'thank you.' "

To all my readers, then—past, present and future—I say: *thank you.*

Tom Wayman
"Appledore"
Winlaw, B.C.
1 January 1993

from
WAITING FOR WAYMAN
(1973)

ON RELATING CALIFORNIA ATROCITY TALES

Their eyes glaze, and thin tongues
slip out to moisten lips.
Faces peer into an imagined sunshine
and palm trees. "Tell us again.
At the height of a party, you coat yourselves
in Mazola oil, lie in a pile, and at a signal
writhe? You have seen clinches between
young men and 50-year-old housewives?
The very rugs steam
at the whispers of the golden sexless
surfers? Men with bleached hair?
Jill marrying John because,
because he has a *truck*?"

The words cackle in their minds.
And long after Wayman has suavely bowed
and dropped South again,
they remember. They remember.
Huddled as close to the border as they can,
they feel a heat drifting up
past Oregon and Washington. They write:
"You said that people there say
California is at most a year ahead?"
They shift uneasily in their chairs,
rubbing their hands together in the cold;
and slowly turn their palms out,
one by one, toward what they hope is Anaheim.

THE PROJECTED POEMS OF LYNDON JOHNSON

I do not think there will be anything about the war.
Some of the titles will explain themselves:
Poem For My Daughter On Her Wedding, or
Thoughts For My Grandchild.
There will be nothing of tides, or the sea.
Poem On My Fiftieth Birthday will consider
achievement, how one learns to live in the world.
Perhaps there will be something of the flatness
of America, seen from an airplane. But perhaps
he would tear that one up.

A series from childhood: how he floated
a raft of old railroad ties nailed together,
sunshine, blue sky, the dust.
And one that matches such with the faces
of two old sharecroppers, to whom
he donated some workclothes.
Scrunched up in the back of a drawer,
an obscene poem about a girl in the Mexicali bullring
riding astride a horse bareback, with a skirt on.

There will be a poem of great peace
about an island where lake water sleeps
and trees sing in a warm onshore breeze,
and finding the skull of a steer on the white sand
after a long dream. And poems about dreams:
discovering his mother had been embalmed
in her casket, when he had specifically asked
that this should not occur. And a dream
about a huge bird, an immense, ordinary starling
with hard beak and claws
atttracted to him because of his name.

These poems cannot be translated.

THE DREAM OF THE GUERILLAS

With their heavy boots, with their old rifles,
with the clear morning of the world in their hands,
*   the guerilleros arrive.*
The guerilleros arrive and they bring the dawn.

—Felix Pita Rodriquez

In the night, in the lonely bed
the dream of the guerillas:
hillsides of vast carnival structures
of steel, whirling me out to a lost handgrip
after my father waits with one leg in
my brother's coffin, whirling,
as a stream of lead hoses a body to bits
under the noise of the nightly warplanes.

The tangle of sheets in itchy skin.
The first guitar notes from
under the floor, with the creak of leather
and the feel of gun oil on their fingers, sweat
under the broad sun, and laughing the windy hair
from their eyes, they stand up;
they are the only men of the age who can stand
kneed in the back, gasping in water,
shot into spasms at short range
they rise, open their books to a clean page
and begin. And of the coolness of her body:
freeways turn in the dark, spinning
a string of lights past huge signs and music
saying: the guerillas, the guerillas are coming
for you, and you must go with them.

And night quiet
after the dream.
Street lights burn on.
The slogans are calm on dim walls. The clock,
the clock says: now
the guerillas are coming and you must go with them.

LIFE ON THE *LAND GRANT REVIEW*

Mad gnome of an assistant editor
Wayman gloats in Colorado
before the mass of manuscripts now his,
his to edit.

Wayman remembers the mounds of his own mail back
marked: "Are you kidding?"
"What is this grunt?" and
"Do us a favor and stick this up your ass?"

Now the tide is turned: all literary America
lies at Wayman's feet; America, with a poet
under every rock. Revenge, revenge,
the very word is like a Bedlam gong
to ring him deeper into rage . . .
"And that's a literary reference,"
Wayman shrieks, slashing someone's poem to
shreddies as he writes rejections
—the same for all: Miss Elsa Eddington Brewster,
editor Riley of the *South-west Pawnee County Quarterly*,
former associates with their cringing, oily letters.
Only the editor-in-chief's friends
give him pause. Wayman weighs
the first-name-basis missives carefully.
Who is putting him on? Who really studied
under Yvor with the boss? Who knew him when?
Who now? Is everybody faking?

Feverish in the cool Colorado evening
Wayman is hammering away at rejecting
faster and faster. The earth heaves,
the business manager elopes,
the editor is arrested in Utah with the funds,
still Wayman is scribbling: "No." "No."
Imperceptibly the word spreads outward
to those in Portland, Oregon and Portland, Maine
stuffing their packages of poems
into the 10 p.m. mailbox slots:
"Wayman," the news has it,

"Wayman's editing in Colorado.
All we can do is submit."

DESPAIR

DOW appears, and the poet Robert Bly, and a building is taken and lost November 1968

I

As though something knew Bly was coming
the night he arrived the first snow began
to sigh wearily down on
the building we argued in
down on the humps in the parked streets,
on houses.
At the edge of town: cold fields
where we found sadness in cabin lights
being forced unhappily out onto the white ground.
We loaded the truck with black boards for
barricades, from the floor of an old silo,
breathing the new winter around us
whispering, whispering down resigned
to the state of things, to itself;
to America, Bly and to quiet.

II

In the black hall of the building
crash of boards dropped, pools of melting snow
and light here and there from passageways.
Hammers. The janitor being talked to upstairs.
We move through the rooms, jam
boards to hold doors tight, lock the big windows,
nail others shut,
slide out the classroom chairs to be
piled one by one against entrances,
tighten wire across wood that could move
to let in the day. But into the flickering noise:
doubts.
"This place is a sieve, we'll never hold it."
"If the police come now or come early
this handful of us is lost for nothing."

And is this where your life changes, your job goes
to another town, the spectre of clubs and gas,
shoving helmets and jail?
The building slows; some faces drift in the hall:
"The place is a sieve, we'll never hold it."
"If we had three hundred instead of thirty, we could . . . ."
"Let's just leave the blockades and go."
Some others go past in the darkness, carrying
a heavy plank.

Again in the open air, I want to learn
depths of commitment or cowardice
crossing the empty streets with some others
to the cold car. What does this leaving mean?
Black flashes of levering a huge partition
against some windows, slumping to a chair, considering:
where does your life change, if not here. Maybe
nothing will happen. What then, but to have learned
what you would do or not do? Footsteps
on the snowy sidewalk leading into the building.
Footsteps out on the ice in the early, early morning.

III

So of all of us who began, fifteen are in custody by noon.
And Bly in the afternoon speaks softly
of a great despair in the land: like the deep snow
out of the lounge windows where he talks, easing down
on the hills and frozen trees. Only fifteen left and willing
to face the massed police and be busted, and Bly
speaks of them slowly, waving his red wristband of support
for the Milwaukee Fourteen, who napalmed draft records
months ago on cement in the sunshine. Bly in the evening
sighs as a wind, his sweet voice soothing
and crackling like a gentle fire in a grate somewhere
warm against a cold night, saying how much
America longs to sleep, longs to forget its Empire
and the wars of Empire, the hatred of all the men of the world
it can burn but not own. Sleep! Bly cries. Sleep.
And in jail, the others say later, it was too cold

25

to sleep, but I nod in the back of the theatre
mumbling yes, yes
I would love sleep, an end to this testing myself
and my words against plans, against actions, afraid
in movements and struggle where love and trust
are not born yet, too new, too beaten by fear,
guilt, doubt. Sleep, and an end to optimism
trying to cheer myself and perhaps another
with the anecdotes of history: with a certainty and
joy that escaped me, it seems,
in the past night when the bitter bone
of a sure defeat seemed worthless
compared to running away to the daily reverses of
talk. Bly, the winter, and slumber swirl in as a fog
of despair at myself, my retreat from myself.
Where am I now in Colorado?
There is so much snow.

ON THE INTERSTATES

after Snyder and Rexroth

After driving all day I pull into the campsite
tense and worried that it'll be full and
pay my dollar in the ringing quiet
and stand talking a few minutes, uncramping my legs.
Then the short drive to the tent area and
shut down the car for the night.

                      First unpacked
from the heated rear seat is the canvas:
unfold it in the dust   then back
for the hammer and box of pegs.
Four corners staked, the metal centre pole
run in and raised   then more pegs.
Gather wood and chop it; sorted into piles and
the fire begun: water to boil
as the cooking box and cooler are
brought out and opened. Then the rush of the meal
until the last of the hot water
splashes into the instant coffee cup

and the warm porcelain rests in my palms and fingers
between steaming sips. It is dark now: the fire
is dull and feverish in the blackness.
I see Orion lift magnificently
over the still car, as the night wind pushes
a matchbook across the table.
Putting down the cup, I tidy the food things
away   studying a map by flashlight
to see how far tomorrow will be.
I have come nearly 450 miles alone today.
I walk out onto the access road
and find the Dipper, the pole star, North
in the noisy sky. Then turn back
check the car and the firecoals
tie down the tent-flap from within, and ease
into my sleeping bag
to begin the dream of freeways: slow trucks rising
all through the rainy morning country.

POEM COMPOSED IN ROGUE RIVER PARK, GRANTS PASS, OREGON AFTER WAYMAN'S CAR STOPPED DEAD ON THE OREGON COAST IN THE MIDDLE OF A HOWLING RAINSTORM AND HAD TO BE TOWED FIRST TO YACHATS, OREGON, WHERE IT COULDN'T BE FIXED AND THEN ONE HUNDRED MILES THROUGH THE MOUNTAINS TO EUGENE, WHERE AFTER IT WAS REPAIRED AND WAYMAN STARTED OUT AGAIN HIS ACCELERATOR CABLE PARTED AND HE HAD TO RUN ON THE LAST DOZEN MILES OR SO INTO GRANTS PASS AT MIDNIGHT WITH HIS THROTTLE JAMMED OPEN AND SPEND THE NIGHT WAITING FOR THE GARAGE TO OPEN WHICH IS AT THIS MOMENT WORKING ON HIS CAR, OR RATHER WAITING FOR A NEW PART TO BE SHIPPED DOWN FROM EUGENE (AND WHICH GARAGE, INCIDENTALLY, WOULD FIX THE CABLE BUT FAIL TO DISCOVER THAT ALL THAT HIGH-REV RUNNING WOULD HAVE BLOWN THE HEAD GASKET ON WAYMAN'S CAR CAUSING FRIGHTENING OVER-HEATING PROBLEMS THE NEXT DAY WHEN WAYMAN DID TRY TO BLAST ON DOWN TO SAN FRANCISCO)

Let me not go anywhere.
Let me stay in Grants Pass, Oregon, forever.

PICKETING SUPERMARKETS

Because all this food is grown in the store
do not take the leaflet.
Cabbages, broccoli and tomatoes
are raised at night in the aisles.
Milk is brewed in the rear storage areas.
Beef produced in vats in the basement.
Do not take the leaflet.
Peanut butter and soft drinks
are made fresh each morning by store employees.
Our oranges and grapes
are so fine and round
that when held up to the light they cast no shadow.
Do not take the leaflet.

And should you take one
do not believe it.
This chain of stores has no connection
with anyone growing food someplace else.
How could we have an effect on local farmers?
Do not believe it.

The sound here is Muzak, for your enjoyment.
It is not the sound of children crying.
There *is* a lady offering samples
to mark Canada Cheese Month.
There is no dark-skinned man with black hair beside her
wanting to show you the inside of a coffin.
You would not have to look if there was.
And there are no Nicaraguan heroes
in any way connected with the bananas.

Pay no attention to these people.
The manager is a citizen.
All this food is grown in the store.

MELANCHOLY INSIDE ORGANIZATIONS

You begin by loving the corporations.
They betray you. In a fine rain all morning
you walk through the city.
A garage door opens. A man's mouth hangs apart.
you go in.

But his party want everything to be stones.
If something is moving they want to hit it.
Everything is simple. They want to die.
They are overwhelmed by nostalgia
for the days when all Christians were Saints.
They are black umbrellas.

You decide it does not mean anything,
only everything. You stand on the wet sidewalk
reading the deaths of the Panthers.
Drops of water roll from your hat.
A dozen or so others are also here.
You go into the paper together. This time
you are very clear:

I cannot escape relating to knives and forks.
To the cold that comes through windows.
To embroidery, elastic bands,
the jammed rooms of the poor
with their piles of mattresses instead of beds.

To clothing stores. Hammers.
The jargon of automobiles.
The body with its tides of blood and water
which cannot be defined or altered by words.
The blood inside the finger.

The deep silence of houses all afternoon.
Gulls. The rainy sea.
Bags of food carried into kitchens
leaving as bags of scraps, crushed packages
and shit. The kind of homes with plants
growing in sunlight on the windowsill.
Sideboard cabinets with glass fronts.

How water is lifted in a bailing tin.
Wet earth. All clutter, and the people
who live in it. Trying on dresses.
Pulling damp air far back in the nostrils.
Relating to forks and spoons.

WAYMAN IN THE WORKFORCE: URBAN RENEWAL

Neil, Brian, Jeff, Rick, Mark, Steve D., Steve W.,
Swede, Tom, Richard, Abe, Bill, and Mike, too.

Forty feet over the floor, on a shaking scaffold
Wayman is in the workforce.
After eighteen years of education
Wayman is out cleaning bricks.
But as he peers down from his wall
knuckles white where he grips the guardrail
Wayman sees through the winter dusk
there is something inefficient
about modern industry. He realizes
everybody is drunk.

There are the gyproc-ers. Passing each other nails
beer and sheetrock, they hammer the boards
onto the framing. And over the windows.
Across the doors. Through the plumbing.

Tapers are working behind them. John Senior
lies sprawled at the foot of a ladder
dreaming of Scotch. Smitty is up on it
sanding, reeling about as his ceiling goes round and round.
Mescalito is mudding the joins, pupils large
in the night. He mutters spells against goodness
taught him long ago in the grotto in San Francisco
the day he was enrolled as a warlock.
"Tabor! Tabor!" he chants, mud in his evil beard.

Dan the Foreman is out
eating supper at Wing's. Wing's menu is brief:
Persian, Siamese, or Alley meat stew.
Back at the site, the construction boys
sit at the edge of the loft and drink.
They are cursing the owner
whom no one has seen for days.
Peel the plumber is busy installing
shower heads, that later will be discovered
simply to hang in the wall. Unconnected

to anything. Milo the electrician
tests for current. Two fingers go
in each socket. He gives a slight twitch;
there is the smell of burnt flesh.
He notes the results on a clipboard happily,
stumbling among the empties.

Up from the sidewalk come the howl of the bums.
Tonight they have organized: John the Colonel,
Reggie Wheelchair, Montana and the Leopardskin Coat
are together. "Eight cents.
Eight cents for a starter," they call.

And Wayman hears from his perch. Somehow
someone has passed him a bottle too.
High over the building trades, Wayman considers his future.
He wonders if they have brick walls
in the breweries.

DAYS: CONSTRUCTION

Days when the work does not end.
When the bath at home is like
cleaning another tool of the owner's.
A tool which functions better with the dust gone from its
    pores.
So that tomorrow the beads of sweat
can break out again along trouser-legs and sleeves.

And then bed. Night. The framing continues
inside the head: hammers pound on
through the resting brain. With each blow
the nails sink in, inch by blasted inch.
Now one bends, breaking the rhythm.
Creaks as it's tugged free. A new spike
is pounded in.

The ears ring with it. In the dark
this is the room where construction is.
Blow by blow, the studding goes up.
the joists are levered into place.
The hammers rise.

UNEMPLOYMENT

The chrome lid of the coffee pot
twists off, and the glass knob rinsed.
Lift out the assembly, dump
the grounds out. Wash the pot and
fill with water, put everything back with
fresh grounds and snap the top down.
Plug in again and wait.

Unemployment is also
a great snow deep around the house
choking the street, and the City.
Nothing moves. Newspaper photographs
show the traffic backed up for miles.
Going out to shovel the walk
I think how in a few days the sun will clear this.
No one will know I worked here.

This is like whatever I do.
How strange that so magnificent a thing as a body
with its twinges, its aches
should have all that chemistry, that bulk
the intricate electrical brain
subjected to something as tiny
as buying a postage stamp.
Or selling it.

Or waiting.

WAYMAN IN LOVE

At last Wayman gets the girl into bed.
He is locked in one of those embraces
so passionate his left arm is asleep
when suddenly he is bumped in the back.
"Excuse me," a voice mutters, thick with German.
Wayman and the girl sit up astounded
as a furry gentleman in boots and a frock coat
climbs in under the covers.

"My name is Doktor Marx," the intruder announces
settling his neck comfortably on the pillow.
"I'm here to consider for you the cost of a kiss."
He pulls out a notedpad. "Let's see now,
we have the price of the mattress, this room must be rented,
your time off work, groceries for two,
medical fees in case of accidents . . . ."

"Look," Wayman says,
"couldn't we do this later?"
The philosopher sighs, and continues: "You are affected too,
    Miss.
If you are not working, you are going to resent
your dependent position. This will influence
I assure you, your most intimate moments . . . ."

"Doctor, please," Wayman says. "All we want
is to be left alone."
But another beard, more nattily dressed,
is also getting into the bed.
There is a shifting and heaving of bodies
as everyone wriggles out room for themselves.
"I want you to meet a friend from Vienna,"
Marx says. "This is Doktor Freud."

The newcomer straightens his glasses,
peers at Wayman and the girl.
"I can see," he begins,
"that you two have problems . . . ."

from
FOR AND AGAINST THE MOON:
BLUES, YELLS, AND CHUCKLES
(1974)

IT IS SEVEN O'CLOCK

It is seven o'clock
When I was a student, this was the hour
by which I had set myself to return to my desk after supper

It is seven o'clock
When I was a laborer, this was the hour
when I had taken my boots off my feet, and was eating supper

Now I have a job where I neither sweat nor think
but wear out my day marking papers with pens and a page of
      instructions

Yet there is always the clock. Twelve hours
and it will be seven again. Eight hours later
I will be back from work once more. Then
it will be seven again:

The hour is pushing me onwards
I am whirling around in its arms
Now it is payday: *here is so much for your time*
Thank you. Goodbye

But something came clear to me once, in the days
when I worked with a board and a shovel: and I say
Wait
Where is the pay for my foot, for its hour of pain
when I trod on a nail you had hired?

Where are the wages to pay my poor hands
which awoke every morning swollen and cracked?
Where can I punch in or punch out
for whatever is lost on the job: for my time after work
too tired to start a new life, for the secret parts of my body:
retina, cartilage, worn down in somebody's service?

Who pays? I sit in a house with a clock, and the house costs
so much a day, so much an hour
Who pays? I eat at the table a workingman's meal
and even the salt has the price on it

And the clock in the house goes around like a coin
till I lie in the darkness, here by the river
and sleep. All night the tugs
hoot at their barges of sawdust and logs
And whatever the weather, for whoever it is at the horn and
        the wheel
my hour to dream is their hour to labor

In the dawn, the riverside mills
groan for fresh rail cars and a change of shift
Here is the whistle that lets off
the hitchhiker, clothes filled with cedar
who during the night, with some others, has turned a whole
        forest
into cash

So it goes. Morning and evening
No hour passes but somebody has traded it for money. Every
        one
someone has bartered and checked and collected
until it seems to me that everybody who works
on shift, off shift, or unemployed
toils in the same huge plant, the Mill of the Earth
that is grinding our lives

I cannot even be sick, doze in my fever
without knowing how much is paid for:
so many sick days permitted with pay in our contract
and so many dazed hours, ill on my own time

And off each hour I work, the merciless actuary
already subtracts so much for my death, an amount
for a frightening accident, and a bit
for my last days out of the ground

Who pays? I pick up a book: what must I do
before I can read it? What does it cost
when I look through the pages at the poems I love?

And this poem: an hour to write out a draft
Who will pay for it? What should
an hour of my life be worth? Or anybody's?

Perhaps if I stand here speaking with you
there is an electrician somewhere, so much an hour
waiting for me to be through so he can go home
Who pays for these minutes? Who?

But when I am ready to despair, because so few will agree
that just for being born we should reward each other
(*congratulations, niece! well done, uncle!*)
with the right to walk around on the earth
with a shirt on, a place to go at night
with food of all sorts on a shelf, until we die

when I am ready to give up
and be yanked round the clock all my days by a dollar

I remember
how every bright season, chemical workers
in the factory of the leaf
effortlessly, without wages, and with everything they want
change sunshine and water into a living thing

and I say
it's that simple, brothers and sisters
it's that hard

It is seven o'clock

WAYMAN IN THE WORKFORCE: TEACHER'S AIDE

Through the late snows of March, Wayman ploughs into the
        parking lot
his car sputtering through the slushy drifts.
Wayman is here to spend hours marking
what the students have scrawled off in seconds between the
        bells:
endless crinkly sheets of Grade 11 English essays.

Only Wayman takes it seriously. Every apostrophe is always
        misplaced.
Every sentence runs on like a television set. One student
        writes
he likes to hang around hippies "because they are so down
        and out
they make me feel positively good." Another compares
a hamburger sauce of ketchup and mayonnaise, oozing out of
        a bun
to "the wounds of a dying soldier".

Some afternoons nobody comes. The classes
simply take the day off. Wayman stays at his desk in the
        library
marking, marking. Every so often
he looks up from his piles of paragraphs
and stares at the empty chairs.

He hears a noise in the quiet. Behind him on the library rug
the Director of English 11 sits, in the full lotus.
He is throwing the I-Ching. "When the students are absent
I have a chance to pursue my hobbies," the Director says
        brightly.
"Did you know that extending the lines of the Star of David
yields the figure of the Maltese Cross?"

Wayman pushes his nose deeper into his papers.
Outside the first green April buds begin, and inside
Wayman begins to sigh. In the spring
his nuts boil over like an old radiator. Day by day
he watches the skirts in the hallway creep slowly up

the 17-year-old fleshy thighs. Breasts seem to swell
under thinner and thinner cotton blouses.
Wayman checks and re-checks his columns of grades.

And on the last day, in June, all the green trees flower.
Wayman turns in his pencils and walks out
past the clock and the picture of the Queen.
He starts his car and drives out of the schoolyard
into the summer. Headed home through the warm afternoon,
      he realizes
he has been marking time.

SECOND-HAND STREET

I

Used plastic flowers, old crockery, a shelf
of torn novels, lamp standards, tables
still grease-stained, with thick enamel
beginning to flake away, fringed
with cigarette burns and stacked
four high. Old kichen chairs
upholstered with torn linoleum.
A fresh chest of drawers of unpainted wood.

And not one of the Street's buildings is new
from the mills on the river north to the inlet docks.
Here and there is a bright facing
of stucco and paint, but the lanes behind
show the rest of the structure: grey wood walls
of suites, tacked on or built over
the street's second-hand stores, Coca-Cola groceries
small electrical repair shops, and the broken coin laundromats
where water seeps out under worn machines.

And if a building was new, as in the neighborhoods
of the Street, it would be a three-storey apartment
with flat roof and modern ornamental iron
and colored lights framing the intercom system
at the entranceway. It would be
constructed of plywood and stucco, with the door frames
made of metal strips painted to resemble wood, with the
        cupboards
hung wrong and mistakes in the plumbing, built
to be serviceable fifteen years, before the small balconies crack
and the windows jam as the foundation settles
and the owner sells and every month
another tenant moves.

This Street runs through its City like an open sore
draining the loads of commerce: highway trailers with huge
        stacks
of cut lumber, or flatbeds of structural steel.

Vans of used parts, towtrucks and the vehicles of small
        printing companies
cablevision installers, furnace oil supply
and local department store delivery. Among these
the citizens' cars sag low on family axles
or rise well-polished over the loud slicks of the roaring boys.

The traffic passes like time, like a wind
out of the sea. An asphalt river of rubber and mufflers
exhausts and gasoline. A sewer of oil changes
and fenders dented or birthmarked with the rust-colored scar
of the work of collision repair garages:
cement block buildings with an overhead I-beam and
hoist, two mechanics, and old tins full of fluid and rags.
A differential resting on the dark workbench, under
the calendar. Empty engine blocks sitting on a patch of grass
        outside.

In the used car lots, the salesmen
sit in the tiny office with their suits and ties.
They stare at the traffic. The stock drips from the day's
        washing;
pennants flutter over the gleaming, patient metal.
The lot lights are on. The signs are all up.
The lot boy has brought them their morning coffee
steaming in the white brittle plastic cups.

II

There is not even the face of hunger
among the people who live along this dam, this moving barrier
across the beginning of the East End. Here is only
the desperation of immigrants, families where the father
works in the millyard, the mother cleans, and both daughters
do shifts after school in the local Safeway. Where all this
        money
is put toward old houses already signed for
that are rented out again to other countrymen: Portuguese
Greek, Chinese, or to the North American young. So even the
        citizens here

are second-hand, belonging to no country but work
and their hour with the lawyer who still speaks
a little of their first language, and is helping them with the
    forms.

All their talk in Canada is second-hand: the children
translate for them to the renters, and if the tenants
have no English or Portuguese either, then everyone stands in
    the kitchen
passing between them the few creased and damaged phrases
they can add to fingers and hands.
The twisting arguments follow the damage money, key
    deposits
and the leak in the gasket of the toilet tank.

And inside
even the air is used. It is filled with the dust
of what has been handled and walked on, rubbed, pushed
kicked open and propped up. Pale green windowsills
and the smell of gas out of the old stove. Refrigerator
and radiators hiss and gurgle to themselves.
And in the deep night, when the land is closest to gathering
    back
the forest's silence, then into the painted wallpaper rooms
comes the thrum and babble of adjoining televisions.
On through the evening hours, the clean blue lines of the
    image
pipe over and over again
the jabbering freshness of something clear and new: a package
    of cigarettes
just opened, where the clean white cylinders
have never been touched, except by machines, and are there
    only for you:

who are watching the screen of a second-hand set
in a room along the Street of a different country.

THE KNOT, THE SNAIL, THE TOOTH

Something I put there stopped the moon's pull:
put a tiny knot in the cord the moon uses
to draw out the thread and cupful of blood.

And the knot held. The moon
only drew water, the tears.

But with infinite majesty, the lords of this life
the moon's agents, secular managers
offered a form to fill out. There was a Friday
a Wednesday, a Thursday and another
Wednesday. Then the string was scraped clean.

There was scarcely time to decide
our eyes in the mirror appeared the same:
what we had killed was a tiny snail.
Yet no one has to change, if they choose
not to kill a snail. So this was more.

All of one possibility for us
we compressed into a pebble, a small white molar
undescended, in the gum.
The tooth was impacted, pressing down on our lives.
A sleep; we had it pulled and thrown away.

Again adrift in the working seasons
I turn the dead tooth in my hand for a compass.
But it cannot show direction, or point me
to anything that will. Through one month like the moon
it had its waxing and waning. Now in my mind
it is a hole in time.

THE DAY AFTER WAYMAN GOT THE NOBEL PRIZE

The day after Wayman got the Nobel prize
he discovered the problem was still there:
how good are his poems?
The poems that are not particularly staggering, or new
to him, or the one that is a terse masterpiece in the afternoon
and is empty by nine o'clock that night.
Always the clean page and the words, the English words.
And what for?

Not to mention the rent, if no difficulty now
as Wayman unfolds the strange cheque from Sweden
then in a month or so, when the landlord drops by again.
And the car needs plugs and points.
And there is the lovely round body of the beautiful woman
Wayman has never been able to touch.

Like the Monday after the Revolution
when we were told to drive to work as usual
so on the morning after a little success Wayman still
can't help knocking the sugar over as he reaches for coffee.

The day after his acceptance speech was published
and again after his reading in Carnegie Hall
Wayman began to wonder
about the day after death.

THE BANFFIAD: THE SILENCE THAT IS LIKE A SONG

I

Rundle Norquay Sulphur Sundance
and the Bow, names of the mountains and the river
stand in the language of my country like a poem:

the high valley, memory, the shape and form of the words
of these huge stones, cold air, and water

Their names do not show how things are, but
on signboards and maps tell
how they were: Crow's Nest, for the survey crew
following the flight of the bird through a pass, or
Kicking Horse, the river named for another moment
long ago, or Tunnel
chosen for what was to be built there
in the mountain, at the townsite
but the scheme abandoned early.

It is easy to forget what they mean.

II

Take a space in the air on the earth.
Wrap it in steel. Put us
inside and hurtle it
a thousand miles along the surface
on a smooth asphalt highway. We are off

down the roads that are the roots of this country
winding and stretching themselves, that bore and twist
into the heart. Somewhere a single moment
appears in the memory, what the road brought
in the trip or dream
of the road, hurrying, tracing the turns of the
white line, on the route from the East:

two outcroppings towering over the highway, a deep cut
the road moves us through, brings us the bird
crossing above

in a dream, in a dream's time
traveller's time

until past Calgary, the mountains deepen
as they do heading in from the West, on the long climb
from Revelstoke, we enter the Kingdom

III

In these highest ranges, the trees assemble.
They stand along the slopes, and across the flat
river valleys, pilgrims under the immense shrine of rock.

They stand for generations. Patient multitudes of trees
crowded together, raising their reverent young, quietly
        enduring.

They suffer the roads men build through them;
the great fires.
They suffer being destroyed for timber.
They suffer ingratitude: the lodgepole pine
provide shade necessary for the spruce to grow
which eventually will displace them.
And animal famine: elk and deer in the 1940s
ate black holes in the alder bark all through these valleys.

Still they stand, under the Continental peaks. Like a city
that appears before some huge cathedral, petitioning
for the benediction of a saint or King, the trees
await the Revelation of the massive stone.

And among these, the rivers go on with their work
building the small deltas of gravel and sand
calling the shores, the river banks into themselves
tipping the closest trees in
and flowing on, under the mountains.

There is also the sound. High alpine wind. The sound of the
    cold, of the air
rising like a flag of air, a blanket of air lifting and falling
in the river of air, the pine-tops make, the sound of the
    mountain.

River of green pine, river of alder, river of blue-green water:
the forests are clear. Like air
like pilgrims, they have simplified themselves
emptied themselves of undergrowth, so every trunk
rises straight and visible into the air. Below
are only their young, and the grasses
and low bushes: bear berry, a flavor
and preservative for pemmican, buffalo berry
ground for a sauce or gravy to eat with the animal
and juniper berry, edible, with the taste of gin.

IV

If only the townsfolk, the visitors
became a less petty people, this would be a Sign.
But they are as busy as anyone
circulating questionnaires on the attitudes of the tourists
or worrying at automobile radiator hoses, rain gear
and the prices of souvenirs. The children
are trained to lie, to service the customers for money.

Radios babble on in the campsites.
Under the solemn trees, the aura of everyday rises
and drops, voices, the roar and putter of engines.

And the trees stand with the wind moving into their highest
    branches
and going, the sound of their valley
will outlast ours. Whatever we do
they rule us, at last we are still but the trees
rise on their air, sighing the breath
that is life to us, the silence of wind. They go on.

They have not noticed us; they go on
in their wind or are cut down, but they have not noticed us.
What is there to see? Their sound will bury us.

Stand in the forest like a tree. What does the forest reveal
when we enter it? What can we read
in the mountain? Only here and there on the trails, others
have left the messages we can stand before, and believe:

"Each large tree exhales hundreds of gallons of water a day.
      This moisture
forms a protective blanket over the forest, moderating the
      weather."

But beyond that, we can go
where the paths lead: the cave of the hot springs up Sulphur,
the wide meadows under Tunnel's cliffs, alongside the Bow,
wet rocks in Johnston Canyon
where the waterfall may be seen through a hole worn in the
      stone.

But what they mean, the nods
and polite greetings on the trail,
what we can hear, is lost.

We pass on. In the silence
the wind is lifting into
the silence that is like a song

V

These are not the words of one who lives
in these mountains, but of one who wants
to put together words as complex and astonishing
as a rock or a tree:
words that are like these, out in the world
not put away somewhere in a cupboard.

Yet how much work goes to make a single tree:
the tangle of hidden roots, the visible monument

of the trunk, its intricate network of cells
and the sap and bark, the branches, the miracle of the leaves.

And each tree stands among thousands, each with this work
     to it.
How do people see it? A tree. What of the rock, too
is forgotten, left out, what cannot be said?

I want to make music on these stones, play
these forests and rivers. And to make the sound of the wind
that is no sound, that is not a single word, rising

in the air

THE COUNTRY OF EVERYDAY: LITERARY CRITICISM

"He was in a hurry," Wood said, "the young foreman
only 26, down on his knees at the base of
the heavy lamppost, impatient to push it back on the block.
He was yelling at the rest of us to give him a hand
and didn't see the top of the pole, as it
swayed over and touched the powerline.

"I was looking right at him. There was a flash
and he just folded over onto his side and
turned black: his ears melted.
There were two holes burned in the pavement
where his knees were. Somebody started giving him
mouth-to-mouth, and I said *forget it. I mean, he's dead.*"

And there are poets who can enter in
to the heart of a door, and discover the rat inside us
that must be kept caged in the head because it is perfectly
      sane.

There are poets who claim to know what it's like
to have a crucifix wedged in the throat
unable to swallow, and how the knot of the stomach
turns into a bowl of fire.

But around and ahead of them
is the housewife endlessly washing
linoleum, sheets, fruit dishes, her hands
and the face of a child. And there is the girl who stands
in the cannery line twelve hours in season
to cut out the tips of the fish.
For the paper they tear out to write on
is pulled from the weeks of working graveyard
and all the weariness of millwork, the fatigue
of keeping it going, the urge to reclaim the body
for the hours not working or sleeping
when the body ends too tired for much but a beer and a laugh.

Beside every dazzling image, each line
desperate to search the unconscious

are the thousand hours someone is spending
watching ordinary television.
For every poet who considers the rhythm
of the word "dark" and the word "darkness"
a crew is balancing high on the grid
of a new warehouse roof, gingerly taking the first load of
        lumber
hauled thirty feet up to them.

For every hour someone reads critical articles
Swede is drunk in a bar again
describing how he caught his sleeve once in the winch of an
        oil rig
whirling him round till his ribs broke.
And for every rejection of a manuscript
a young apprentice is riding up on the crane
to work his first day on high steel.
"Left my fingerprints in the metal
when I had to grab a beam to get off," he says.
And Ed Shaw stands looking down into the hold
where a cable sprang loose lifting a pallet
and lashed across the dock, just touching one of the crew
whose body they are starting to bring up from the water.

When the poet goes out for a walk in the dusk
listening to his feet on the concrete, pondering
all of the adjectives for rain, he is walking on work
of another kind, and on lives that wear down like cement.
Somewhere a man is saying, "Worked twenty years for the City
but I'm retired now."
Sitting alone in a room, in the poorhouse of a pension
he has never read a modern poem.

THE COUNTRY OF EVERYDAY: WORKPLACE

The defeat of any jobshop: dusty windows
and a long scrape down the cement of one wall.
These will not be restored unless the company collapses
or moves, and the new owner decides to paint.
Each day, now, the same smudged interior.

This is the inside of a building no one will ever love.
It is like a mine shaft thousands of feet under the earth:
a place we only descend into for labor.
The broom misses the corners. Dirt
grows on the tops of the baseboard heaters.

The place fills with the sadness of anything
herded together, with a weariness
like the sound of the noon hooter
or the foreman's whistle, pushing us back on the site after
     lunch.
The room is tired of being kept awake all night.
One shift is the same as another.
Even if the fluorescent lamps are shut down
this room in the darkness holds only work.
That is all it has known: nothing else
will ever be brought out of this mine.

Even the demolition crews will be sweating
as their crowbars start to pull the wiring from the walls.

DEAD END

Feeling morbid in the Spring, Wayman figures
it's time to get ready. He pours himself another coffee
pads over to his desk and begins.
If I should die, think only this of me:
There is some corner of a field somewhere
That is forever Wayman . . . . It strikes him suddenly
this has been done. He tries again.
The laws of probability tell us
that every breath we take contains some molecules
from the last gasp of Julius Caesar. Think about that.
At this very moment you may be breathing
some of Wayman's too . . . .

This seems awfully long-winded. Wayman recalls a friend
who refused to read anything longer than a page.
And a newspaper editor who howled at him:
"If you can't say it in a paragraph, forget it."
Remember me this way, Wayman decides:

Say of Wayman's end, as he said himself
of so many unfortunate things that happened to him while he
lived:
At least
he got a poem out of it.

from
**MONEY AND RAIN:
TOM WAYMAN LIVE!**
(1975)

THE BLUE HOUR

The blue hour begins
on the North Shore mountains
flows down to the harbor's edge
and into the blue blanket of City.
This evening the air has turned
a deep marine blue, that settles over the roads and houses
street lamps and neon, muting the detail of
telephone poles, trees, and the angle of roofs
so the low hills of blue become the ground swell
to a blue anthem, points of light everywhere across it
the ten thousand notes of a song: chorus of downtown
and West End, then the long verses of Kitsilano,
Marpole, Mount Pleasant, Grandview
and the far reach to Capitol Hill.

The color calms the blue water
stretching west past the flashes of Point Atkinson's light
and threads in again among
the tugs and sawdust barges
headed slowly up the Fraser's still north arm.

In this hour, a bus
which has blazed the name of my City
across half a continent
rolls in at last with its riding lights burning
moving up the Oak Street Bridge through the blue air.

CUMBERLAND GRAVEYARD, FEBRUARY 1973

I stand with one hand on the wet uneven rock
that marks the grave of Ginger Goodwin
at Cumberland cemetery in the drizzle of
a Wednesday afternoon: a meadow hacked out of the rainforest
littered with old and new stone markers,
grey cement slabs, and the damp mounds of fresh earth.

In the rain, Cumberland graveyard
looks like the one on Kaien Island where I grew up
in the shadow of Mount Hays, where people said
*I'd hate to be buried there and have rainwater
trickling down my back forever.*

But they got buried anyway. And here
there are not so many graves as I thought
considering the long chain of coalmine disasters
that ran south from here seventy miles, for nearly
one hundred years. There are few markers that say
Killed in an Explosion in No. 4 Mine; Aged 17 years.
When people get around to putting up stones
they don't seem to care how death arrives, but carve:
Only Sleeping; *Lo, I am with you always*; and *Gone Home.*
Lots of the graves are neglected now—not as abandoned
as the Chinese cemetery half a mile up the road—
but inscriptions have worn away, headstones tilted
and cracked, and here a slab of old pebbly concrete
above some graves shakes as you walk on it. A few of these
    slabs
have sagged and split open. You can crouch
and peer in, but inside is only the top of more wet earth
and a few broken plastic flowers
blown across and down from the more modern graves.

A strange familiarity appears in the plots marked
Gran, or *Papa, Mama and Mary*, or
In loving memory of our son Tommy, when now
no one can make out the surname. And where the graves
are clear as the Hudson family's, say
—infants, children, parents and the last date in the 1950s—

what would bring anyone out in this rain
to stand looking at the letters chiselled into the blocks of
      soaking stone?

But Goodwin's grave differs from these.
Not that it's by itself, on the contrary
you could just about get another one beside him
but the rest of the way around he's completely hemmed in
and there's a new pile of wet earth not ten feet away.
Yet Goodwin seems buried
for another reason that these: nobody bothered to put
his birthdate on his stone, for example,
just that he was *Shot, July 26th, 1918.*
And the lettering isn't nearly as regular
as on the other stones: *Lest We Forget* it says
and it's about as professional as a title
someone has put on a pamphlet they've printed
overnight, trying their best with the letters
but not doing so well, and the whole thing soon forgotten
anyway. On the top of the stone
is a crude sickle and hammer—done
as though in the years before there were Commies,
when those who thought a certain way were sure
that what had just happened in Russia
had something in it for them. Like the words
it's an amateur's job: the sort of sickle and hammer
someone might carve if he'd only heard about it
or seen it drawn by hand on a piece of paper. Under it all
in place of a slogan, it says *A Worker's Friend*
like a dog is man's best friend, except the worn cement curb
that outlines the grave is exactly the size
of a man, not so small as a child or as large as a family.

The afternoon I was there, the grooves in the rock
that form the words were painted black, with fresh red color
for the verb "shot" and the symbol above.
And that's the secret to this wet grave, this poem
and the dripping old coal town: somebody there
drops by once in a while to see how this rock
bears up under the weather. Maybe only one old man
an ex-miner who lives on in this valley

where the trees have covered the slag heaps and hills
but are going themselves higher up, missing
in vast swathes cut across the mountains. One old man
in the rain and maybe nobody knows exactly who
and won't until he dies also and then two graves
will decay together, or maybe only one
because who puts up stones for old miners now
when the last mine closed twenty years ago
and no one can say when the old man last worked anyhow?

But right now that oldtimer
is keeping a dream going.
Strange to think of a town like Cumberland
having a dream, after all the lives squeezed from it
—in just a second underground
or in unendurable years and days and hours
aboveground and down, all the grinding horror
of living a Company life for a Company lifetime.
But we know it was Cumberland's dream
at least for a day, becuse everyone says at that time
a mile of the town appeared to bury Goodwin:
a mile of miners and women and kids
which is a lot of people to bury anybody
especially if they aren't being paid to do it.

Strange to think of a town like Cumberland
not only having a dream, but a hero:
an honest-to-something hero (I don't see
how I can call him less
since he came out of nowhere particular
that anyone knows, and worked in the mines
and struck in the strikes of '13
when the great Canadian militia
terrorized the coalfields for a year, before going off
to die like pigs in the muddy barnyard of France.
And Goodwin meanwhile
didn't kill anybody,
kept working away for a better life
up at Trail, became secretary of the miners there
fighting conscription while he could
and when Blaylock and Cominco wanted him dead

64

or out of there at least, he went—
though on his own terms—hiding out here
until he was shot in the back for it.).

And Goodwin didn't kill anyone
to be a hero, not even a scab or a German
or an Indian, as far as we know, but he thought
and read and he wrote, and he talked to people
—we know all that—and he went to lots of meetings
and probably called too many of them himself.
But because he could do all these things, he was a little
    different
than the man beside him, but he was anyway, really
—that being the way thing are—though this difference
plus having a sort of dream
landed him flat on his back under this rainy meadow
a little earlier than his consumption likely would have gotten
    him here.

And that's all. I walk out of the graveyard gate
as he can't do any more, and cross the wet asphalt
to the car. He's behind us now, like being wakened in the
    night
and having the dream you were in hesitate in your mind for a
    second
then slip down through a hole in the net of the night
and vanish into the solid dark wall of black air.
That dream is lost, what it was forgotten
unless, even years later,
you start another dream in which suddenly you are aware
this is a dream you began once before.

WAYMAN IN THE WORKFORCE: ACTIVELY SEEKING EMPLOYMENT

Everybody was very nice. Each place Wayman went
the receptionist said: "Certainly we are hiring.
Just fill out one of these forms." Then, silence.
Wayman would call back each plant and corporation
and his telephone would explain: "Well, you see,
we do our hiring pretty much at random. Our interviewers
draw someone out of the stack of applications we have on file.
There's no telling when you might be notified: could be next week
or the week after that. Or, you might never hear from us at all."

One Thursday afternoon, Wayman's luck ran out.
He had just completed a form for a motor truck
manufacturing establishment, handed it in to the switchboard
        operator
and was headed happily out. "Just a minute, sir," the woman
        said.
"Please take a seat over there. Someone will see you about
        this."

Wayman's heart sank. He heard her dialling Personnel.
"There's a guy here willing to work full time
and he says he'll do anything," she said excitedly.
Around the corner strode a man in a suit. "Want a job, eh?"
        he said.
He initialled one corner of the application and left.
Then a man in a white coat appeared. "I'm Gerry," the
        newcomer said.
"This way." And he was gone through a doorway into the
        plant.

"We make seven trucks a day," Gerry shouted
standing sure-footedly amid a clanking, howling, bustling din.
"Over here is the cab shop, where you'll work. I'll be your
        foreman.
And here is the chassis assembly . . ." a speeding forklift
        narrowly missed them
". . . and this is where we make the parts."
"Wait a minute," Wayman protested, his voice barely audible

above the roar of hammers, drills, and the rivet guns. "I'm
     pretty green
at this sort of thing."

                              "Nothing to worry about," Gerry said.
"Can you start tomorrow? Monday? Okay,
you enter through this door. I'll meet you here."
They were standing near an office marked *First Aid*.
"We have to do a minor physical on you now," Gerry said.
"Just step inside. I'll see you Monday."

Wayman went shakily in through the First Aid office doors.
"I need your medical history," the attendant said
as Wayman explained who he was. "Stand over here.
Thank you. Now drop your pants."
Wayman did as he was told. "You seem sort of nervous to me,"
the aid man said, as he wrote down notes to himself.
"Me, I'm a bit of an amateur psychologist. There are 500 men
in this plant, and I know 'em all.
Got to, in my job. You shouldn't be nervous.
Remember when you apply for work you're really selling
     yourself.
Be bold. Where are you placed? Cab shop?
Nothing to worry about working there: monkey see, monkey
     do."

Then Wayman was pronounced fit, and the aid man escorted
     him
back through the roaring maze into the calm offices of
     Personnel.
There Wayman had to sign for time cards, employee number,
     health scheme
and only just managed to decline
company credit union, company insurance plan, and a
     company social club.
At last he was released, and found himself back on the street
clutching his new company parking lot sticker in a light rain.
Even in his slightly dazed condition,
a weekend away from actually starting work, Wayman could
     tell
he had just been hired.

THE FACTORY HOUR

The sun up through a blue mist
draws its own tide: this is the factory hour.
As I drive east, I pass dozens like myself
waiting on the curb for buses, for company crummies,
for car pools; grey plastic lunch buckets,
safety boots, old clothes. All of us pulled
on the same factory tide.

                    The plant's parking lot
is the dock; the small van of the industrial caterers
has opened at the furthest gate through the fence: coffee,
        cigarettes,
sandwiches. Walking in through the asphalt yard
we enter the hull of the vessel.

The great hold is readying itself for the voyage. Steam
rises slowly from the acid cleaning tanks
near the small parts conveyor and spray booth.
We pass to the racks of cards; sudden clang of machine shears
but otherwise only the hum of voices, generators, compressors.
Click and thump of the cards at the clock. The slow movement
of those already changed into blue coveralls.

The hooter sounds, and we're cast off. First coughs
and the mutter of the forklift engines.
Then the first rivets shot home in the cab shop's metal line.
Air hoses everywhere connected, beginning to hiss, the whir
of the hood line's drills. The first bolts are tightened:
the ship underway on the water of time.

Howl of the routers: smell of fibreglass dust.
Noise of the suction vacuum, the cutter, the roar
of dollies trundled in for a finished hood. And the PA
        endlessly calling
for partsmen, for foremen, for chargehands:
Neil Watt to Receiving please, Neil Watt.
Jeff Adamanchuck to Sheet Metal.
Dave Giberson to Gear Shop . . . to Parts Desk . . .
        Sub-Assembly.

The hooters marking the half-hours, the breaks,
the ship plunging ahead. The PA sounding
Call 1 for the superintendent; *Call 273*; *Call guardhouse*; *Call
    switchboard.*
Lunch at sea: sprawled by the hoods in ordinary weather
or outside at the doors to the parts-yard if fine; whine of the
    fans
and the constant shuttling of the forklifts
show that the ship still steams. Then the hooter
returns us back to the hours of eyebolts,
grilles, wiring headlamps, hoodguides, shaping and
sanding smooth the air-cleaner cutouts. On and on
under the whir of the half-ton crane, rattle of the impact
    wrench,
grating of new hood shells as they are dragged onto a pallet.

To the last note of the hooter: the boat returned to its City.
A final lineup at the timeclock, and out through the doors
to the dockside parking lot. Late afternoon:
I drive into the tide of homebound traffic, headed west now
still moving into the sun.   ᵂ

NEIL WATT'S POEM

At first metal does not know what it is.

It has lived so long in the rock
it believes it is rock.
It thinks as a rock thinks: ponderous,
weighty, taking a thousand years to reach
the most elementary of hypotheses, then hundreds more years
to decide what to consider next.

But in an instant the metal is pulled into the light.
Still dizzy with the astounding speed
with which it is suddenly introduced to the open air
it is processed through a concentrator
before it can begin to think how to respond.
Not until it is hurtling along on a conveyor belt
is it able to inquire of those around it
what is happening?
We are ore, is the answer it gets.

A long journey, in the comfortable dark. Then the confusing
noise and flame of the smelter, where the ore
feels nothing itself, but knows it is changing
like a man whose tooth is drilled under a powerful anaesthetic.
Weeks later, the metal emerges as a box full of bolts.
What are we? it asks. *Three-quarter-inch bolts.*

The metal feels proud about this. And that is a feeling
it knows it has learned since it was a stone
which in turn makes it feel a little awed.
But it cannot help admiring its precise hexagonal head
the perfectly machined grooves of its stem.
Fine-threaded, someone says, reading the side of the box.
The bolt glows, certain now it is destined for some amazing
        purpose.

Then it comes out of its box and is pushed
first into a collar, *a washer*, and then
through a hole in a thin metal bar.
Another washer is slipped on, and something

is threaded along the bolt, something else
that is made of metal, *a nut*, which is whirled in tight
with great force. The head of the bolt
is pressed against the bar of metal it passes through.
After a minute, it knows the nut around itself
holds a bar of metal on the other side.

Nothing more happens. The bolt sits astonished
grasping its metal bars. It is a week before it learns
in conversation with some others

it is part of a truck.

ROUTINES

After a while the body doesn't want to work.
When the alarm clock rings in the morning
the body refuses to get up. "You go to work if you're so keen,"
it says. "Me, I'm going back to sleep."
I have to nudge it in the ribs to get it out of bed.
If I had my way I'd just leave you here, I tell it
as it stands blinking. *But I need you to carry your end of the
    load.*

I take the body into the bathroom
intending to start the day as usual with a healthy dump.
But the body refuses to perform.
Come on, come on, I say between my teeth.
Produce, damn you. It's getting late.
"Listen, this is all your idea," the body says.
"If you want some turds so badly you provide 'em.
I'd just as soon be back in bed."
I give up, flush, wash and go make breakfast.
Pretty soon I'm at work. All goes smoothly enough
until the first break. I open my lunchpail
and start to munch on some cookies and milk.
"Cut that out," the body says, burping loudly.
"It's only a couple of hours since breakfast.
And two hours from this will be lunch, and two hours after
    that
will be the afternoon break. I'm not a machine
you can force-feed every two hours.
And it was the same yesterday, too . . . ."
I hurriedly stuff an apple in its mouth to shut it up.

By four o'clock the body is tired
and even more surly. It will hardly speak to me
as I drive home. I bathe it, let it lounge around.
After supper it regains some of its good spirits.
But as soon as I get ready for bed it starts to make trouble.
Look, I tell it, *I've explained this over and over.
I know it's only ten o'clock but we have to be up in eight hours.
If you don't get enough rest, you'll be dragging around all day
tomorrow again, cranky and irritable.*

"I don't care," the body says. "It's too early.
When do I get to have any fun? If you want to sleep
go right ahead. I'm going to lie here wide awake
until I feel good and ready to pass out."

It is hours before I manage to convince it to fall asleep.
And only a few hours after that the alarm clock sounds again.
"Must be for you," the body murmurs. "You answer it."
The body rolls over. Furious, and without saying a word,
I grab one of its feet and begin to yank it toward the edge of
       the bed.

THE OLD POWER

The old power is still here: pulling into work one morning
to find the access road to the company parking lot
jammed with men and vehicles, more cars
piling up behind, spilling out onto the main street
and down adjacent lanes, everybody arriving
from different directions to stand together
at the gate of the almost-empty lot
(just a few foremen's cars and the night shift of painters)
where five men from the company's sales and service division
on strike for more than a month now
stand with their picket signs.

Early morning dark, and a cold rain.
Five men with sheets of cardboard looped around their necks
changing feet to keep warm, drinking coffee
from the small white cups somebody brought them:
five men in a line, occasionally talking to someone else
but mostly just standing at the very edge of company property
and then a little space
and then all four hundred of us, mixed in
with our lunchpails and boots and the cars that brought us
      here.

Like an old myth that is suddenly alive: a marvellous event in
      a forest
that happens to you personally so that again
you can believe in what you once had clung to
and then abandoned: five sheepish men
in the rain at the end of a road
hold back our hundreds. And this is something
both of us make: they carrying the symbol out in front of us
and we agreeing. So whatever happens here
is ours.

After half an hour in the drizzle, the sky getting lighter,
not a supervisor or foreman in sight,
some of us wander off to the Lougheed Hotel for coffee.
Then, I drive home. And all the while the five men stand there
like pillars of the old power, an idea made flesh,

an idea that works. So that today, Thursday,
no one has to build a single truck

and we can take all the rest of this day in the rain
for ourselves.

VIOLENCE

The cars leap out of the plant parking lot
lay rubber, fishtail, and disappear.

Bill says: "The scar? When I was up in Ashcroft
I was coming out of the pub one day and a guy I'd never seen
smacked me in the face with a piece of wood.
Broke these teeth and split me open along here: nose, lips,
    chin.
I got stitched up, and the next day
had a buddy drive me around town looking for the guy.
I saw him, told my buddy to stop
and leaped out holding a tire iron behind my back.

"The guy recognized me. He comes up and says:
'I'm sure sorry about yesterday. I thought you were
    somebody else.'
I said to him: 'You have three seconds to start running.'
He turned to get away, and I let him have it across the back of
    the head.
Cold-cocked him right there in the street.
Then I kicked the shit out of him, broke a couple of his ribs
and me and my buddy got out of there fast."

And Magnowski, the giant partsman, on his wedding night:
"They put shaving cream, lather, all over my car.
I stopped in at a garage to wash it off
and as I was using the hose the attendant comes out
and just stands there, making all these dumb comments
like: 'I guess you're really gonna screw her tonight, boy.'
I couldn't believe it. He was big, but
I'm a head taller than him. I was going to deck him
but it was our wedding night. Debbie was right there in the car
and I'm wearing a tuxedo and everything.
So I just said: 'Do you have a hose with some *pressure*
in it, asshole?' He got kind of choked up at that.
He could see I was really mad, just holding myself in.

"But I didn't want to ruin it for Debbie on our wedding.
I think I'm going back this Saturday and see if the guy is still on."

And Don Grayson, another partsman, limping around
with a broken foot he got kicking someone
in a fight in the Duff beer parlor.
He and his friends took exception to some remarks
that were made about the woman who brings the food.
And me always careful not to get in a fight.
Chris and Ernie, Bucket and Phil at lunch one day
talking about a brawl, and me saying:
"It takes two to fight. If you don't want to
you can always walk away." And Ernie really horrified
at this: "Oh no, Tom, no, no.
There are times when you have to fight, you just have to."
And me maintaining that you don't
and everybody looking disgusted at my idea.

How is it I have clung all my life to my life
as though to the one thing I never wanted to lose?

Bob changes the subject. We begin to talk about car accidents.

THE DEATH OF THE FAMILY

"You married, Tom?

No, but the girl I'm going with is.
To someone else. Ha-ha. You see . . .

But they aren't listening.

"Tom, I was going with a woman
for two years. A few weeks ago she asked if I was going to
    marry her.
I told her I might some day, but, hell,
I was married all those years
and once I got my divorce I'm not in any hurry to do it again.
I didn't say I wouldn't *ever* marry her.
I just said I didn't want to right now.

"She says to me: 'Dave, if you don't want to marry me
I'm wasting my time.' And that was it.
I tried to call her up a couple of times
but she said if I didn't hang up she would hang up on me.
Bang. Just like that she stopped seeing me.
I think she's crazy. I know she hasn't been seeing anyone else
but she'd rather sit at home and see nobody
than go around with me anymore if I won't marry her.
I just want someone to visit after work, to go dancing with.
And there's something else: she once told me
if we got married, she would come first.
She meant, before my kids. I have two, and there's her three
but she says she has to come first.
There's no way: my kids come first with me.
Who else is there to look after them?"

And young Bob
over from Cab Build for the morning, to help out when we're
    behind:

"My Mom walked out on us twice.
After the first time, when she wanted to return
my Dad he took her back and it was okay for a while.

Then she left again. And you should see the guy she went off
    with:
a drunk and everything."

                      Then through his mouth
the voice of his father: "We treated her like a queen
but it wasn't enough for her."

All over the plant, through the long hours.
Up to Test to replace a grille's side shell, I hear Jim Pope's
    steady voice:
"When my first wife left me, I phoned in to take the day off.
I had the locks changed by ten o'clock, and was down to the
    bank
to make sure she didn't get a cent.
Then I went over to check about the car registration.
You have to move fast when it happens . . . ."

Someone in the small group of coveralls
is receiving advice.

THE KENWORTH FAREWELL

Everyone wore eyeglasses for safety.
To Wayman at first the factory had the look
of a studious crew of graduate students
dressed by mistake in torn and baggy coveralls
who had wandered in through the high aisles of stacked parts
to stand aimlessly amid the machines and assembly stations.

And the boys in Cab Build
were hooting: *Whoop. Whoop.*

Settling in, getting to know the place, Wayman discovered
both box-end and open-end wrenches, fine- and
     coarse-threaded nuts.
Also the forklifts, which never failed to release
a warm fart of propane when Wayman passed behind them.
And Wayman meanwhile got real intimate with his wristwatch:
staring at each minute in every hour
until somehow it turned into a morning, and even an entire
     day.

And the boys in Cab Build
were hooting: *Whoop. Whoop.*

Wayman returned home each late afternoon to the rebirth of a
     bath:
the grand feel of fresh clothes against his skin.
Picking the dirt out of his nose, he understood
not only was he in the factory, the factory was in him, too.

So he learned all the Kenworth slogans:
"It's only a truck", and "It's only a Kenworth",
and "At sixty miles an hour, who is going to know the
     difference?"
Also: "There's a right way, a wrong way,
and a Kenworth way." And Wayman mastered
the Great Kenworth Fault Game: "It isn't *my* fault."
Even if an error took only a minute to fix
like forgetting to drill safety light holes, for example,
everyone argued happily for hours

all the cosmic questions and implications
of each other's ultimate innocence and guilt.

Wayman learned the faces, and what each meant.
Working with young Bill was a rain of washers
he and Larry endlessly tossed back and forth.
Wayman discussed women with so many, only to later discover
they were just out of high school and still living at home.
And there was the day Gerry the foreman complained about
        the quota:
"I have seven hoods to get out today, but what do I have
to do it with? A hunky (meaning Daniluk)
a hippie (meaning Wayman)
and a God damn sky pilot . . ." (meaning Wayne
who before Wayman left finally cornered him
and gave him one pamphlet on the Four Spiritual Laws
and another called—Wayne said: "Don't worry about the
        title"—
Jesus and the Intellectual).

And the boys in Cab Build
were hooting: *Whoop. Whoop.*

Wayman might have stayed forever.
But his first clue was a Monday morning
when it seemed the weekend had never occurred.
The second clue was Paul Palmer telling him
(Palmer the mainstay of the Pipe Shop's
Hose Amputation Division):
"I've worked at this bench a year, but it feels as though
I might have been here one day, or always."
And so often the great gleaming $50,000 trucks
wouldn't start at the end of the Final Line
and had to be towed out into the yard—which broke
        Wayman's heart.
Also there was a moment when Wayman found himself
in his own car rolling down the highway near Bellingham:
heading north again on a Sunday, but driving just the same
on that beautiful concrete freeway which he knows also drifts
south in a dream towards California.

So Wayman at the end picked up his toolbox
shook hands with the foreman
and walked out another time through the Kenworth Keyhole:
that man-sized door set into a truck-sized door
on which someone has thoughtfully painted "Door".
Wayman passed out of the world of tires and fibreglass dust,
timeclocks, and the long sessions upstairs in the can.

And as the boys in Cab Build
howled their last farewell: Wayman
was on his way once more.

THE CHILEAN ELEGIES

1. Salvador Allende

The wood comes from a living tree
brought down, ripsawed into rough boards
and nailed together into parts-boxes and forklift pallets.

Dust has settled onto the battered wood:
a heavy dust, from metal that is drilled and pounded,
from fibreglass that is cut and shaped, and from the weariness
of the hands and legs that have done this day after day.
Eyes have looked at this dust every lunch break
and at our ten minutes mid-morning and mid-afternoon.
Dust from overtime, and carried in
on the wind from this factory's City.

Allende is dead. I have not followed the newspaper
for three years: the news is what happens to me.
Now he is dead another layer of dust,
black grains, has sifted in among the stacks of truck parts.
The dust makes a faint sound as it settles
like a man who sighs, far away. I believe Allende's dust
is falling into every factory in the world.

It says that whatever you might want
there is no reason to vote. Men are alive who are killers
and not a word or a vote anywhere can stop them.
If you love your life there will never be change.
This is one more thing the poor know
in every factory. And now Allende is with us
in the dust on the concrete floor.

2. Neftali Reyes

*"Pablo Neruda" was the pen name adopted by the young
student-poet Neftali Reyes.*

This does not mourn Pablo Neruda.
I speak here the death of Neftali Reyes.

83

Neruda goes on in the ocean of words
that is his life forever. Certainly he was stopped
before he said everything, but in that
how is he different from anyone else?

But Neftali Reyes is dead.
He died of a cancer called The Modern Army:
a cancer present in every country. In Chile, in Canada, an
        Army
day after day is patiently training to kill.

That is all it is for. It cannot so much as make its own rifles
or run a railroad for very long. And it has no one to shoot
but its brothers and sisters: neither an invasion of Eskimos
nor penguins threatens, and against the wars
of the U.S. or Russia what could it ever attempt?

Yet in each state, the President or Governor
keeps the uniform of the High Command in his closet.
Sometimes he wears it only on special occasions
but often enough it is pulled on each day.

As it was on the final day of Neftali Reyes.
He was one of a thousand *chilenos*
struck down that day by the Army. And like each one
suddenly pulled into the sea of death
his mouth filled with so much salty blood
that for once and for the last time it was blood, human blood
that poured over his lips and chin instead of a song.

Neftali Ryes is dead. But the great wave that broke over him
was scarcely a ripple to the sea Neruda
moving on the Neruda earth. Despite the deaths of so many
the death of Neftali Reyes, as with the lives of so many
the life of Neftali Reyes

Neruda sails on with his cargo of poems, with his freight
of coffee, bathtubs, typewriters, carpenters
grasses, electricity and the poor: goes calmly on
through space, carrying the living and the dead
carrying the dead body of Neftali Reyes

carrying the dead body of Neftali Reyes

on the great Earth: pablo neruda.

3. Pablo Neruda

It was as if a cruel winter
descended on the coast of Chile
locking the water and soil
into a vise of snow and the cold.
Somewhere in the white emptiness
near what had been Valparaiso
an immense glacier moving down from the mountains
calved an iceberg with the sound
first of a pistol shot
and then a colossal groaning and thundering
that echoed and echoed all over the frozen world.

Falling away from the seaward edge of the glacier
the iceberg, in its second of birth
shot huge plumes of water high in the noisy air:
the calling of seabirds rising for a thousand miles.
The ice bobbed once, settled comfortably into its marine
        existence
and began travelling steadily. Against every current
every belief that in books is considered natural law
the iceberg floated north. Crossing the Pacific equator
it shrank some, but grew again as it passed the mists of
Oregon, the heavy rain of the Washington coast.

One afternoon it appeared at the end of my street.
When I returned from work, a small crowd
stood at the doors of my apartment building
talking about it. Like an advertising campaign
it was not unexpected: we have read so much
by certain navigators
about these matters, that when at last the iceberg floated
here in the harbor off Kitsilano Point
how could I be surprised? And it has come up Yew Stret
climbed the stairs to my room

and knocked on the door. It has entered my blood
and started up the hot streams of my arteries
melting toward my heart.

Growing on top of the ice
is one tiny rose, imperfectly formed, a rose
that can only grow in the dirt
but nonetheless is alive on the ice.
When the iceberg enters my heart
I think only the rose will be left.

And it is the rose that will stay
in my heart forever.

4. Larry Tetlock

And where it says *they shot so many factory workers*
does it mean Larry Tetlock
who began at this factory three months before me
after the usual adventures working for Sears
hanging drapes: trying to install new white ones
with a spiral screwdriver someone had loaded with oil
and having his van catch on fire
from a faulty battery one day while making deliveries?

Is this who they mean? Larry, at 20
with a brand new Vega to drive and working
to pay for it, intending to look for another job
if we strike, fed up with the din of this one?

Or is it Ernie they killed? Ernie, who jumped
from the Hungarian Army in '56, learned English
and used to work at General Paint?
Thirty-six and divorced, he was back to Hungary twice
and realizing he would work at the same place here or
     there
elected to stay with racetracks, stereos, and all the movies he
     can see?
"I'm always happy," Ernie says, one day
when everybody is angry at him for being so dense.

86

"I never get depressed. No." Why do they want
to put an end to his jazz collection, his nights
in the Ritz Hotel beer parlor?

But these aren't the men who have died.
These will be back at work Monday, and Tuesday, and also
        Friday
firing Huck bolts and lifting their end of the fender
until they quit and get another job
or until I quit and sit in a room writing lines
until I too get another job. Not Vancouver, but in Santiago
in those rainy graveyards surrounded by old houses
partitioned into suites, family areas, and rented rooms
fresh earth is dug, and a sound of crying
a shriek, and a heavy silence goes on
for entire avenues, so many people put into the ground
like fill for some seedy construction project
involving the mayor, his uncle the contractor, and the pay-off
of a number of zoning officials and building inspectors.

Except that it's death. What do they think a man understands
who works in these places, a man only the newspapers
and certain theoreticians of the Left consider "a factory
        worker"
a man who believes himself simply to be his own name
—Larry Tetlock, for instance? Why does an order go out for
        his death?

What if the first thing he knows about bullets
except for a friend who has offered to take him hunting
is the bullet inside his own head that the Army intends
to let him keep forever? What do they think he sees
that they want to sever the optic nerve
so what the eyes take in will never get to the brain
and from there to his hands?

Why cause this disruption in production:
no end of trouble and rescheduling for
foremen and chargehands, not to mention whole families?

Why should they kill Larry Tetlock?

5. The Interior

The smell of potatoes just taken out of the earth.
The problem every carpenter faces, where the wood
nearly fits. The man who secretly wants to leave his wife
and only his fantasies keep his sexual life alive.

These things no government can alter or solve.

The lineup in the small bank branch on East Twenty-ninth
after work on Friday: old boots and the shapeless trousers,
short windbreakers whose sleeves end in hands that clutch
the paper that means life. Other lines
that have worried their way into the faces above the eyes.

These mean an ache for money that lasts an entire lifetime
from busfare each morning through to the tiny pension.
These mean it is luck that rules: the wisps of lotteries, horses,
or entering the pool each payday for the best poker hand
that can be gathered from the company's number on your
        cheque.

Also, applying when they're hiring: no government
has been able to touch that.

The small towns of the Interior. The railroad towns deep in
        the forest.
What has the government to do with them?
The struggles of the young teacher
who has arrived to work in the school
mainly of Indians. All the arguing
with the principal, and with the old librarian,
the enthusiasm carried into the desperate classroom.
And the Indians themselves. Their new hall
they built themselves at Lytton, which had to be boarded up
after a month because of the damage. The summer camp
they built twenty miles away in the mountains
where a young boy drowned the second week it was open.
It too is abandoned again to the silence.
Potato chips and Coke the staple food of so many.
And television, television, television . . . .

On the Thompson River, or in Parral
the government is not the government of the Indians,
not of the young teacher, not of the townspeople,
not of the lover, the carpenter, the man who digs potatoes in
    his yard.

But where a government
takes the remotest of steps
to return home to the ground, and even this small gesture
is embargoed, denounced, plotted against
and at last some incredibly expensive aviation gasoline
is pumped into certain jet fighters donated by another
    government
existing thousands of miles away
there is a loss that goes deeper than the blood,
deeper than the bodies put into the ground,
that descends to the roots of the mountains
and travels that far down in the crust of the planet
along the continental chains
until all over the world another sorrow is confirmed
in the lives of the poor. Once again
we are made less. There are men and women
who in the cells of the fibres of their being
do not believe the Indians are dying fast enough
do not believe the poor are dying fast enough
do not believe that sickness and hunger,
automobile crashes, industrial disasters
and the daily suicides of alcohol and despair
are ridding the earth of us with sufficient speed.
So they call for the only institution
maintained at the highest possible level of efficiency:
the men with guns and capbadges, willing or conscripted,
whole armies and the tireless police. These are the men
who have made of this planet throughout my life
a vast geography of blood.

*So many shot for subversion in Temuco. So many arrested
for drunkenness in Lytton.*

And there is not a government in the world that wants to
    abolish the factory.

CODA: A Chilean Incident

Two soldiers are lifting a dead man
out of the rubble of a factory.
They have lashed together a tripod and are winching the body
up through a hole of shattered concrete, splintered wood.
The factory was Chilean, bombed by the Chilean Air Force.
The men alive are Chileans, as was the dead man.
It seems to me there is no such thing as a country:
there are men and women, and there are also men and women.
The lines into the wreckage are taut now:
the dead man is almost up to the surface.

And after they have brought him this far
they go on lifting him. The people who work at the Civic
        Morgue
say they were cautioned not to reveal how many bodies arrived
and what happened to them, under penalty of arrest
        themselves.
But they say that after dark, load after load of bodies
were transferred into Army helicopters
which lifted off, lights blinking, into the noisy night
headed steadily west. Once out at sea, beyond Valparaiso
a door was opened in the side of the aircraft
and the cargo dumped into the air.

That instant over the Pacific
is as high as the Army wants to carry the dead man.
As they gave him his death, so they give up his body
to the long fall through dark wind, and the water.
A dead man descends through the blackness, through the
        white spray
of the sea's surface, and deep into the colder, darker ocean
wrapped in an Army shroud. He falls
further than any winch made by anyone in any factory
ever can lift him out now.

THE RETURN

The poet comes back.
After the agony in the great stadiums
suddenly converted into prisons:
the torture of the young woman
in the corridors under the bleachers,
the rape and beating of the journalist's wife
while he is watching, the daily executions,
the electrode making contact again and again
on the body of the mechanic strapped face-up on the table:
its black point darting in like the tongue of a snake
now searing the scrotum with terrible pain, now the tip
of the penis, now the inside of the lower lip,
the nipples, the tongue, now the eye is forced open
and the electrode brought down toward the pupil . . . .

After his body is stilled, the poet returns.
He knows that no one jailed the former Ministers of Health
when the new government began for the first time
to distribute milk to the poor.
But the hands of a woman who worked in that program
now never stop shaking.
No one wished to interrogate the local executives
of a foreign mining company
about the long years of sorrow and sweat wrung out of Chile.
But there is a miner who lay on the concrete and bled inside
from the kicks of the police, until he died.
And no one sent for a squad of torturers from America
to investigate those Americans found living in Santiago
after the election. But a certain unit of the Brazilian military
instructed in the American school in Panama, and in their own
        country
flew in to begin processing their countrymen
discovered after the coup to have previously fled into Chile.

And there is a woman who heard so much screaming
she can no longer utter a sound.
There is a body dropped from an Air Force truck
into the street of a slum, that only on close examination
can be seen to have been a woman.

But the poet comes back.

His breath, his voice, his book
once again begin journeying.
His country goes down again
into the horrible night of its continent
but the poet continues to move.
Everywhere he comes to the poor like a man in trouble
and is taken in or not depending on their nature.
Those who receive him risk everything
just as though they hid again the living fugitive
but, as before, when he leaves he departs as their friend.
Those of the poor who are fearful, and turn him away
go on being poor, being frightened, still waiting
for the miraculous knock on the door that they know
will one day arrive to show them a better life.

The poet goes on. His words
are specks of light gleaming out of the darkness.
Death surrounds us all, but his words
go on speaking out of the blackness.
Hunger still sits in the stomach
like an egg soured into a chemical burning in the guts.
The muzzle of a gun is still pressed against the head of a man
who is shot before he can say a single syllable.
The voice of the poet is powerless to stop this.
The man who is beaten, his front teeth
snapped off under the sticks of the police
—he, too, loved the sound of the fresh salt wind
pouring in continuously over the waves of the sea beach . . . .

But to everyone left numb
in the silence between these cries of agony and despair
the poet's voice goes on talking, calmly, persistently.
Also through the long drudgery of a lifetime
it keeps offering to those who have lost them
the words that mean a gift of the earth.

The poet says: "They burned my house in Madrid,
the house of flowers, geraniums, and a green horse.
The pulled down my house at Isla Negra,

brought down its great ceiling beams carved with the names
of dead companions, lowered my flag: sea-blue, with a fish on
 it
held in and let free by two chains.
And when I saw the house of poetry was destroyed again
I knew that poetry now would be most needed elsewhere.

"So I began travelling. When I was alive
I took my place in the struggle. Now I am dead
my voice still speaks, ringing like a vast silence
which is really a mouth, filled up one by one
by those who take up my cry, which is their cry,
sounding our words together, drowning out torture
and the police, louder, drowning out hunger and fear,
louder, drowning out sickness and want, louder and louder,
speaking our life on this planet as loud as we can
until at last we drown out death."

THE KISS AND THE CRY

When we first kissed, that November night
I heard the faint noise of crying.

I drew away my lips. In the cold air
someone was sobbing.

She pulled me back to her. We kissed again, mouths opening,
tongues beginning their first discoveries
of where the warm blood goes, pulsing, inside our flesh.

But the crying grew louder. Through my ears
I recognized the tears of the woman I had just broken up with
after two years. And without opening my eyes
I heard her joined by the hoarse masculine agony
that must be the husband of the woman I clung to now
—arms around the bulky fur and cloth of our coats—
the husband she had left six months ago.

Kisses and kisses. But the cold night around us
grew an avalanche of crying: the tears of her parents, and mine
for what we had done and what we intended. Tears added on
by those friends of ours who were bitter and lonely this
        evening
and the crying of others we didn't know who were likewise
        alone.
Tears of the City's married:
how none of their lives were like this moment,
tears of those worn out today at their work,
tears of the crippled, retarded, tears of the mad,
the strange broken tears of the hungry, the sick,
and the effortless, hopeless, continual tears of the poor.

All this surrounded us, where we clutched each other in the
        night:
a howl and clamor filling the empty street
and the chill air. And I could pick out
the sound of myself crying: painful, uncontrollable gasps
of my chest and breath, spasms driven by some hideous loss
I had not yet discovered . . . .

In the front seat of my car, where we embraced like
      adolescents
hands moving desperately over each other's bodies under our
      heavy winter clothing
though both of us nearly thirty,
I addressed the sound of so much misery:

If my sorrow added to yours could help, I said
I would give up joy.
I swear that, if I could, I would go right now to live in a
      different world:
some planet without this constant unhappiness.
But I no longer believe my pain
will help another human being.

And when I said this, there was not a sound in the car
or under the street lights, except her breathing and mine.
I was very calm, very certain.
I think at that instant another person was born.

from
FREE TIME:
INDUSTRIAL POEMS
(1977)

INDUSTRIAL MUSIC

for Michael Millar, Michael Taylor, Gary Walsh

After a hundred years they paused
and they heard
music; other things were on the wind
but they heard a music filling in the continent behind them:
their own music, which grew slowly,
starting at the quietest moments
like a flower, or at prayer, and at
work, and then beginning to be pumped through
cash registers, radios, and finally even leaked in
through small grilles in elevators.

But as fast as the melodies get smoothed
into a dollar, a man stands up in a noisy bar and
begins to sing, and another man joins him and
another, until the air is filled again with music,
human voices. And twenty thousand of us
are put in a single vast room
to hear one famous voice with a song rise through amplifiers
and the songs also come from just Bob Garrison
driving his '55 Willys up the Canyon from Siska
on a rainy Saturday and only me and one other
jammed into his front seat listen.

And I remember in the truck factory Boris Hukaluk drumming
everywhere, standing in Cab Electrical
tapping out the intricate rhythms with his wire stripper
and a screwdriver, but Boris also
knows everything about Folding Hoods after years
working at that before, so he gets assigned back on the days
Hoskins doesn't show. And I asked him there
why he didn't ever become a professional musician and he said
I didn't like the life; too many late nights all the time
so he drums weekends in a cabaret, in the house band
without even a name, and does special jobs at New Year's and
drums through his days and years at the factory
his fingers and pencils falling on the metal. One day
were are up at Test fitting a hood and one of the mechanics

picks up Boris' rhythm and sends it back to him
with his wrenches, as best he can, and Boris
grins and stops what he's doing and gives out
another short riff, and this time
a couple of guys try to match him, and Boris laughs
and taps out another complicated run
and this time maybe half a dozen guys start
clumsily pounding away after his lead. And this makes so
    much noise
(since somebody is banging on a waste can) that the foreman
comes out of his office to find out what's up
but sees Boris and shakes his head and goes back.

Then it's lunch and someone turns a truck radio on, and the
    music,
rock now, pours into the echoing Test bays
like the wind when somebody rolls aside one of the huge doors
on a cold wet February morning, the wind
flowing in off the river among the parked tires and motors,
the tool boxes, air hoses and containers of oil,
a wind that carries with it all the sounds of the City at work
this day: grudgingly, but alive, and moving.

FACTORY TIME

The day divides neatly into four parts
marked off by the breaks. The first quarter
is a full two hours, 7:30 to 9:30, but that's okay
in theory, because I'm supposed to be fresh, but in fact
after some evenings it's a long first two hours.
Then, a ten-minute break. Which is good
another way, too: the second quarter
thus has ten minutes knocked off, 9:40 to 11:30
which is only 110 minutes, or
to put it another way, if I look at my watch
and it says 11:10
I can cheer up because if I had still been in the first quarter
and had worked for 90 minutes there would be
30 minutes to go, but now there is only
20. If it had been the first quarter, I could expect
the same feeling at 9 o'clock as here I have
when it is already ten minutes after 11.

Then it's lunch: a stretch, and maybe a little walk around.
And at 12 sharp the endless quarter begins:
a full two afternoon hours. And it's only the start
of the afternoon. Nothing to hope for the whole time.
Come to think of it, today
is probably only Tuesday. Or worse, Monday,
with the week barely begun and the day
only just half over, four hours down
and 36 to go this week
(if the foreman doesn't come padding by about 3
some afternoon and ask us all to work overtime).

Now while I'm trying to get through this early Tuesday
        afternoon
maybe this is a good place to say
Wednesday, Thursday and Friday have their personalities too.
As a matter of fact, Wednesday after lunch
I could be almost happy
because when that 12 noon hooter blast goes
the week is precisely and officially half over.
All downhill from here: Thursday, as you know

is the day before Friday
which means a little celebrating Thursday night
—perhaps a few rounds in the pub after supper—
won't do me any harm. If I don't get much sleep
Thursday night, so what? I can sleep in Saturday.
And Friday right after lunch Mike the foreman appears
with the long cheques dripping out of his hands
and he is so polite to each of us as he passes them over
just like they taught him in foreman school.
After that, not too much gets done.
People go away into a corner and add and subtract like crazy
trying to catch the Company in a mistake
or figuring out what incredible percentage the government
has taken this week, or what the money will actually mean
in terms of savings or payments—and me, too.

But wait. It's still Tuesday afternoon.
And only the first half of that: all the minutes
until 2—which comes at last
and everyone drops what they are doing
if they hadn't already been drifting toward
their lunchboxes, or edging between the parts-racks
in the direction of the caterer's carts
which always appear a few minutes before the hooter
and may be taken on good authority as incontrovertible proof
that 2 o'clock is actually going to arrive.

And this last ten minute break of the day
is when I finally empty my lunchbox and the thermos inside
and put the now lightweight container back on its shelf
and dive into the day's fourth quarter: only 110 minutes.
Also, 20 to 30 minutes before the end I stop
and push a broom around, or just fiddle with something
or maybe fill up various parts-trays with washers
and bolts, or talk to the partsman, climb out of my
coveralls, and generally slack off.
Until the 4 p.m. hooter of hooters
when I dash to the timeclock, a little shoving and pushing
in line, and I'm done. Whew.

But even when I quit
the numbers of the minutes and hours from this shift
stick with me: I can look at a clock some morning
months afterwards, and see it is 20 minutes to 9
—that is, if I'm ever out of bed that early—
and the automatic computer in my head
starts to type out: *20 minutes to 9, that means*
30 minutes to work after 9: you are
50 minutes from the break; 50 minutes
of work, and it is only morning, and it is only
Monday, you poor dumb bastard . . . .

And that's how it goes, round the clock, until a new time
from another job bores its way into my brain.

FRIENDS LOGGING

One day I hear them stomp up the stairs,
kick at my door again, and here they are.
Whether because of the winter shut-down, just a few days off,
or because the summertime woods are about to burn
they sit, ask a few questions about my life
and then resume logging: the chainsaws start up, sawdust
    begins flying,
the air of my room fills with smoke,
the smell of the wet forest, and with the sound
of rigging signals, diesel engines, and the first huge cedar
    toppling.

"Did you hear the one about the little man
—about so high—who comes into camp and asks for a job as a
    faller?
'Here's a chainsaw,' they tell him, 'let's see what you can do.'
I don't use a saw, he says, *I use this*:
and he holds up a little-bitty axe.
'You can't do anything with that,' they tell him
and he says: *Show me a tree you want cut.*
They do, and in three quick blows
the tree creaks, leans, and crashes down.
'My God,' somebody says, 'where did you learn to fall like that?'
You know the Sahara desert? the little man asks.
'Sure,' they reply, 'but there aren't any trees there.'
There aren't now, the little man says."

And that's only speaking with me. If two of them
arrive at the same time, I have to leap under my chair
after less than a minute once they begin to talk to each other
as spruce, hemlock and fir
start dropping to the ground one by one
all over my room. If I go out
for even a few minutes—to get some beer
or something—when I get back
I can hardly push the door open
because of the tangle of branches and roots,
machinery, and the litter of stumps and logs
filling my room like a jumbled windfall.

"There's this chokerman, see, and he saves up enough money
for a trip to Europe. He's flying along in the plane
over Italy, when the pilot comes on the PA
and says the plane has engine trouble
and they are going to issue parachutes so everybody can bail
     out.
The chokerman begins yelling for his luggage,
he wants his suitcase, right now.
The stewardess tries to calm him down
but he keeps demanding his bag, so finally
they get it for him. He opens his suitcase
and pulls out all he has inside:
a frayed, kinked, twisted, horrible-looking cable.
'What use is that?' asks the stewardess.
'The plane is going to crash. You need a parachute.'
Not me, says the chokerman. *This damn cable
will hang up anywhere.*"

Even they admit it is sometimes too much.
Everyone talks about the job after work
but who else but these speak about it night and day?
Steve tells me: "I'm lying asleep, first night back in Vancouver,
when a train goes by and blows its whistle: *hoot*, hoot hoot.
Now that's a logging signal
so I start to dream I'm standing in the wrong place
and this gigantic log is bearing down on me . . . ."

And Mark: "We're sitting in the pub talking
about the number of logs we've yarded that day
and about the most anyone has ever yarded that we've heard
     of.
One of the guys who drives a caterpillar tractor
meanwhile is trying to squeeze past us to get to the can
but nobody is paying much attention.
Finally he says in a loud voice:
*"Do you mind moving your cold deck
so I can get my cat through?"*

On and on: while the waiter re-fills the table,
the hills get barer and barer
and my words spill across their paper, into the common air.

KITCHEN POEM

I put the bacon into the pan.
It lies there, lank and perfectly relaxed.
After a few minutes, though, a marvellous transformation
starts: the bacon begins to whisper, then hiss,
sinks down, becomes transparent, bubbles and snaps
and babbles to itself, turning crinkled and brown and stiff.

Meantime, I cut up some mushrooms.
The knife blade enters the soft puffy white flesh.
What is a mushroom: a fruit? A vegetable?
Inside the cap, as half the mushroom falls away
gills and a tiny breathing space are revealed—
a secret maritime connection: earth-fish, land-anemone
alive in the ocean of the mossy forest floor.
As the mushroom slices are added to the intense heat of the
        pan
each one dries out and appears
as a miniature kippered herring.

Now I drop in the eggs. Two circular wonders.
The clear fluid becomes white and solid
as the yoke builds its own bright dome in the snow.
Personally, I like to put a lid on it all
so the white covers the yoke entirely.

Food is where everything starts. A thin slice of cheese
melting on my tongue. And I *have* to
talk about salads. Water
fleshed into green crisp ragged wafers:
lettuce leaves torn up and put in a wooden bowl.
With sliced celery stalks: one piece crunching
between my teeth as I work. Tangy radish:
a red warning sign of a coat, and below that
an apparently-calm, deceptive interior. Not like the tomato
which is honestly red and juicy all the way through.
Green peppers are even more deceiving:
really you just eat the rind because that's all there is.
To me, peppers seem a little embarrassed when they are cut
        open.

They have spent so much time attempting to look like an apple
that once they are exposed
they try to vanish underneath everything else in the salad.

Avocados. Warm green California memories
shipped all this way for me: a fruit
with a pudding inside, sweet, bland and mushy,
the absolute opposite of carrots
which are delicious edible wood,
staunch and starchy, each carrot disk
slipping off the knife. I pick one out to munch on:
aaaahh.

Then I put my wooden fork and spoon in
and stir the whole pile up. I pour
an oily and vinegary dressing on, slippery and
pungent with spices. Out of the water
and the ground it all comes, to my plate and my fork
and into my mouth.

I eat. Taking the planet as a whole
not very many can do that. Luck
has brought me this food, though something harsher than luck
keeps the others away from the table.
I eat, and go on talking.
Others who can't eat, or who can't eat so much
meanwhile are thinking of something else to say.

But still I love to eat, as a person should.
This is how I know there is something wrong
with those who keep food from the poor.
I think if the vegetables controlled the world
there would be enough for all, since even a vegetable
knows its duty is to feed the earth. Something lower than that
must have its hands on things: some sickness
that decrees some people will eat and not others.

Yet food has its own revenge.
Hugo Blanco says that in Chile, under the generals,
when every form of resistance was mercilessly stopped,
the men with the guns had to allow

people to buy food and cook together
since conditions under military rule made this necessary
if many people were going to eat at all.
Now for this activity you need some sort of organization
Blanco says, and you can't stop people talking to each other
while they're stirring up the soup. And they don't
Blanco says, always talk about food.

See how sneaky eating is? If think if you want to control
human beings, you really have to keep every bit of
    nourishment
away from them. For if someone once opens his mouth to eat,
who knows? instead of rice going in
a word might come out.

Myself, I go on eating, as I go on breathing.
But I hope these two acts are all that ties me in this life
to those men and women who for now decide who starves.

SATURDAY AFTERNOON IN SUBURBAN RICHMOND

Through the front window:
the rest of this street of duplexes.

Inside, between the easy chair
and the sofa, the arborite dining table
and its chairs, the sound of the stereo flows
like the wall-to-wall rug: soft, insistent,
the smooth bland melodies, faint strings,
gently falling choral harmonies repeating
over and over.

        The sound also slides
around the antique wooden chair
refinished last winter in the basement:
its old wood sanded smooth and shellacked.
Windows in the rear of the house
face across the small back yard to a similar dwelling.

These are rooms filled with a vague regret:
like sighs, choices made and accepted.
Each object in these rooms is assigned four numbers:
the date it was purchased, what the price was,
exactly how much was saved in the transaction
and how much the same item would cost today.
These numbers have been spoken of so often
they hang in the rooms like whispers, like sighs.
There are also numbers given
to the entire half of this building.

All night the numbers go on whispering
disagreeing with each other like the merciless arguments
of the television. In the morning the numbers
subside a little, but soon after breakfast they start up again.

The numbers say
this is a place where people go mad.
They tell how one still afternoon, when the woman
sits by herself, when the baby is upstairs asleep,
his plastic tricycle motionless against one wall,

when there is no sound in the house but the low soothing
        murmur
of the stereo, when the dog, too, rests by the coffee table
suddenly the woman rises, moves into the kitchen
and begins to yank open drawers.
She dumps their contents onto the floor:
cutlery, cooking utensils, bits of string,
her old notebook stuffed with recipes torn out of magazines
and cards left by various home-repair agencies.

Cupboard doors are pulled ajar; her hand and arm
shovel out dishes and plates so they smash
first onto the kitchen counter and then
drop to shatter in the litter piling up on the linoleum floor.

The baby upstairs is wakened by the noise.
He begins to cry. The dog
becomes excited: he barks wildly as
cans of soup and infant food,
tins of peanut butter and flour are hurled into the mess.
The doorbell rings: it is the paperboy here for his monthly
        collection.
The woman does not answer: she rips open packages and
        boxes
of powdered desserts, orange juice,
oatmeal and sugar and empties the contents into the air.
The telephone rings: it is a rug-shampoo salesman
calling to announce that the woman will win a prize
if he is allowed to demonstrate his product in her home.
The telephone, too, is disregarded. The woman
is digging with both hands in the interior of the refrigerator:
milk bottles, eggs, fresh celery and boxes of fish-sticks
fly out into the room around either side of her body.

Then the woman stops. She picks her way through the debris
and sits down at the kitchen table. She stares
through the kitchen window across the back yard. Outside
everything is very calm.

Perhaps when the husband comes home, he agrees to move.
The place is put up for sale. The numbers
whisper hollowly to themselves in the empty rooms until
the new owners arrive. Then the numbers change
but the faint hissing goes on.

The new people, too, one day sell their part of the building.
And of all those who ever sleep in this place, not one
will recall with fondness the rooms and items
which made up their life in this house. It is as though
a kind of death is in these rooms: no one
wants to remember they were alive here.

WAYMAN ASCENDING INTO THE MIDDLE CLASS

In the middle of a trans-Canada excursion
while he visits for a week with the parents of a friend
Wayman lies in a hammock through the hot August days.
Far behind him now are the horrible winter mornings
he got up in the dark and dragged his lunchbox off to work.
Here, as he sips a drink in the gently rocking couch
scarcely a thought crosses his mind about his old companions
still probably stumbling about complaining as they
hammer nails, steer tugboats
or chase logs through the bush a thousand miles away.

A light breeze springs up. Through half-closed eyes
Wayman contemplates flowers, and a leafy screen.
He begins to sway into sleep. The beer bottle
slips out of his languid grasp
and falls almost silently onto
the thick green lawn.   Wayman sighs.
He feels himself float
in his hammock, and begin to drift upwards:
ascending, as he snores
into the middle class.

HIGHWAY 16/5 ILLUMINATION

South-east of Edmonton, on the road that leads
to Vermilion, Lloydminster, and the Saskatchewan border
I feel coming into me again like
a song about a man born in the country
the joy of the highway: the long road

that reaches ahead through these wooded rises, the farms
that spread their fields out around themselves
flat to the sun, the odor of hay filling the cabin of the car

mile by mile, border after border, horizon
to horizon. The highway stretches away
in all directions, linking and connecting
across an entire continent

and anywhere I point the front wheels
I can go.

GRANDMOTHER

In a house in Fresno, the television
lives with the family like a grandmother from the father's side.
She is up with the wife at six, when the baby daughter cries:
a grandmother willing to help, awake, but silent:
what she thinks flickers across her face without a sound.
While the father sleeps, the mother sits with the grandmother
feeding the baby: the eyes of the wife lift above the spoon
from the face of the child to the face of the silent grandmother.
The day outside begins to fill
with the sun of palmtrees; birds
call again and again from the high branches and leaves.

When the older child gets up, he stands at his doorway in
      pajamas
to stare at the familiar scene: his mother, grandmother
and the new baby. All day long in his play
in and out of the yard, the house, his meals and the steady sun
he goes back and forth by his grandmother
as she talks to herself, inwardly, her thoughts visible
but noiseless. In the afternoon, when the father wakes
the grandmother speaks to the older child for a while.
The parents glance toward her themselves now and then
as if to hear what she says. And once in the warm evening
the telephone says that the maternal grandmother
across the city is watching something on her own television
she thinks the child might like. All eyes
go on the grandmother, who begins talking again at once.
But the young body loses patience with the old
and she is left to address the empty California air.

Late at night, when the baby and the child are in bed
the parents gratefully turn to the grandmother.
When the mother goes on into the bedroom
the father listens to grandmother alone.
Then she is quiet, while he has his music
but her thoughts still pass restlessly across her face. At last
in the very early morning, the father says goodnight to the
      grandmother
and goes in himself to sleep. The grandmother sleeps,

the father sleeps, the mother sleeps, the little boy sleeps.
The baby turns fretfully in her crib, and cries out.
But there is no answer, and she sinks again, sighing,
back to her warm and milky infant's dream.

WAYMAN IN QUEBEC

It began simply enough, as an invitation
for Wayman to spend a few days at a lake
in the Laurentians, but as soon as Wayman's car
crossed over the bridge at Hull, what's this?
the trees along the highway suddenly became
"les arbres" and a house
"une maison" and Wayman was relieved to see
the familiar face of Colonel Sanders
revolving reassuringly, but, wait,
below his customary goatee, the Colonel was now selling
"les poulets frits à la Kentucky".

Wayman felt he should be able
after all those high-school tests he had endured
to inquire politely as to where he was going:
"Bonjour. Où est la direction à Chénéville?"
or something like that, but his heart sank
at the last moment, and all he could stutter out
was "Chénéville? Chénéville? *Keep going the way you're
    headed*
a calm voice comforted him. *Turn left at the next set of lights.*

So he was off through the traffic again
or maybe he was "parmi les autos" or that might be
"les voitures d'occasion" as the signs had it.
Anyway, driving along with "la rivière" gleaming away
behind the riverside farms, that is, "les fermes"
all this time Wayman was considering
How do you say Wayman *in Quebec?* and also
What am I doing here?

RAINY NIGHT ON THE 401 HEADED WEST ACROSS HASTINGS COUNTY

After midnight, rain on the windshield and the highway.
Returning from Kingston, we go down and rise again through
    the wooded darkness
ascending and dropping away according to the gradient of the
    road.
Every few miles, trucks have parked on the shoulder: cabs and
huge boxes of the tractor-trailers, some with their clearance
    lights on,
others just black shapes and reflectors in the dark.
Occasionally two trucks will stand together
motionless at the crest of a hill.

But usually they park alone: dozens of trucks
asleep by themselves at the edge of the freeway.
A few cars still travelling like this pass them, and also
hundreds of other trucks that haul all night through the rain.

This evening in Kingston, so many men and women
made me feel happy about my poems.
I want to say to each one: it is for you
they are written, if they please you.
When you like them, it is as though
I have been made welcome again on the earth.
Who else in their thirtieth year has known such pleasure?

I think of the men and women speaking to me
who have made me feel they are with me, with what I do.
Under my hand, the car drives in the storm
through the night of the sleepers and the trucks that keep
    going.
When we get to Toronto, it will be half past three, the streets
    wet,
still raining.

I am glad I was born.

SUGAR ON THE RIM

*Rub the rim of a coffee mug with a lemon. Dip the rim
into sugar. In the cup add 1 1/2 to 2 oz. of brandy and
fill with coffee. Top off with whipped cream to which
vanilla and sugar have been added.*

1.

After hours of love we paused
and she brought
a mandarin orange, ice-cold
in the pocket of my palm.
Lying back on the soaked sheets
I felt the heat rise from our bodies
sweat slick along bellies and legs
and I took off the chill peel of the orange

and placed one cool section of orange-flesh in my mouth
where my teeth burst it open
pouring the cold orange water
over my tongue and throat.

2.

One man works here for a hundred acres of land
at Houston, B.C., and his hope for a mobile home.
Many, many put in their hours
in the slow climb out of debt for new engines,
three-speed transmissions, radial tires
or condominiums in Surrey. There is one I know
who works for one hundred and forty dollars take-home
laid fresh in his wallet on Friday in new twenties and tens
for the bars, the clubs, the restaurants
of the weekends and evenings of his life.

But I have worked here the last fifteen days
full of her shy smile of pleasure whenever she sees me stare
    at her

and close, close, when she kneels naked over my body
and our brown eyes catch again, and fingers
stroke fingers and hold tight for a moment
before our flesh and her breath go mad.

3.

From over the dim cocktail-lounge tables to her bed
of rich yellow sheets and a thick yellow quilted comforter
high up in a white apartment, white fur rugs on the floor
and a kitchen of orange placemats, small appliances, quiet
     music:
she is that smooth, as her long round limbs
clear white and lovely, her careful clothes,
that going down by elevator the first Saturday morning
to my car, I felt I had begun
some perfect movie affair, as though I too
was in smooth fashion with the time.

But outside her building, as the memory of her beautiful face
began in the cold air, I saw
around each eye as it laughed, tiny lines
that said she belonged to the earth: to be loved

like a season.

4.

But there are others she is fond of:
she is away, drinking in the ski lodge after her lessons;
she cannot see me Friday night.

Then in spite of everything I have become
a horror moves through my streets.
It is the ogre I have wrestled with so many times.
Alone in my room I become a tiny man:
black and crisp, like an obsessed flake of ash.
Only with great effort can I stand up
and go downstairs into the real air.

There I put on my coat of experience
which says *possession is the poison of love.*
It says *all you can ever have of her*
is what the two of you have
when you are together.
There are no chains of paper or words
to bind two people forever. For the sake of your life

do not destroy what you have
out of anger and fear for what you might not get.
Laughter and pleasure
must fill those minutes you have with her.

5. Winter Rain

The east wind, that is so strange
in this City by the western ocean,
drove the rain against the window.
And in the night, while I was in her
tears formed at the edges of her eyes and moved
out across her face, and I stopped

and it was confusion, she didn't know
how she should feel about me, should see me so much,
she felt responsible, and didn't want to, didn't want
me hurt with the pressure and guilt that would mean
for her, she wasn't sure if she should begin again
what ends so badly every time.

And as she spoke I felt all the weight
of my body on hers and shrank and came out.

Later the rain swirled against the glass,
dripping onto the sill. No other sound.
Out of a long embrace, in the dark, we made love.

6. Winter Rain II

Am I to have you, then
only by chance, as when the winter rain
sounds some nights at the window?

7.

Ah, but what weeks it was for rain that winter:
the cold water poured down all day, and after work
my legs would be wet to the skin just walking
a block or two to the store, my coat
drenched through and chill on my back,
not drying for hours. And at night
the winter rain outside, passing through
her misted window, was a tropical downpour
filling the room, a hot
dampness everywhere, bedsheets and pillows sodden
by the green ferns, steaming, water pooled on our bodies,
mouths damp
with mouthfuls of the hot wet flesh, wet hair, mouthfuls
of warm rain.

And the cold only began in the early morning
when I came out into the street again to meet
the chill drizzle of the following day.

8. Christmas

She's gone three weeks at Christmas; the rainwater
runs down the glass: some of the moving drops stick

for a minute, others
collect the still drops they touch
as they trickle down the pane: moving, stopping, flowing on

as her fingers moved sometimes
on the sides of my body, my ribs

three weeks: in the tree heavy with dripping tinsel
green lamps dye the green needles near them a softer green,
glowing with a still, steady light.

9. The Holy Hour

Lying with her in this bright room
on a sunny morning

or after dark, in the dim light just before sleep

I come into a holy hour: out of the rush of a life
this is the hour I am still,

satisfied. This morning

we lean back on the bed's pillows
holding the mugs of hot sweet coffee
warm in our hands.

WHERE I COME FROM: GRANDFATHER

A dead man. A dead person,
who ran away from the London Jews and joined
the Royal Sussex Regiment, shipping east
in an old three-decker to India, his pay-book
stamped *Church of England*, under his new
English name. The Regiment
taught him grammar and arithmetic
while he garrisoned the North West Frontier,
had the collar of his uniform shot off,
and was promoted to corporal, but one night
an officer returned to camp drunk
without the proper challenge, so every NCO on duty
—including him—got reduced to the ranks.

Back in England, they say he and his brother
stood in Trafalgar Square and tossed
to decide who would go to Canada and who to South Africa.
Thus my grandfather was awarded Toronto
and a job as a machine operator
for Tip Top Tailors, a wife, a family,
a death, and another wife,
a house on Borden Street eleven-and-a-half feet wide
in a street of Jews, with Jews living upstairs.
He also got a strike, in the midst of the Depression
and only went back to his machine during
another war. In 1945 he was chosen
Inner Guard of the Mozirir Sick and Burial Society
—a social and self-help club for ex-Russian Jews
which he was too, if you went back far enough
though locally he was known for his speech and military
        bearing
as "the Mayor of Borden Street" or "the Englishman".

In his last years, he refused to give up the house
though he was sick a number of times, and though
the street began to fill with south Italians.
A kid from the neighborhood prepared a meal for him most
        days
in return for a little money. And his room

began to hold all the clutter and dust of the single elderly poor:
faded snapshots and photographs, a calendar, the same few
    dishes
used every day, a television continually muttering
and mumbling to itself, the bed rumbled and half-made.

When he died, few on the street knew him.
He had to be carried into death by
a step-cousin's band of musicians
who had attended the funeral out of courtesy
and stayed to bear the old man to the grave.
They lifted him into a small shed at the edge of the cemetery
and came out and stood around, while shards of porcelain
    were put
on his ears, eyes, nose and mouth
to show that in the grave nothing is heard,
nothing seen, nothing smelled, nothing tasted
and nothing said. The first handful of sand from the grave
was put into the coffin, to show
earth to the earth.

                    And standing at the open gravesite
the young rabbi with the red band in his hat
who never knew any of us in life or death
but managed anyway to make up a little message about my
    grandfather
which actually could have been about anybody
now led my father in the halting, word-for-word
repetition of the Kaddish.
Then they turned on the machine for lowering the coffin
and flung a mat of synthetic grass
over the slowly descending box, as inside
what was left of what had been my grandfather went down
wrapped in the step-cousin's shawl.

Seven days the candle burned for him: seven days
seven years ago now. And from my grandfather
I got my father, my name,
the ring they took off his body that he had been given
when he made Inner Guard, and I got
a cheap disposable yarmulka handed out from a tray

at the funeral, a skullcap I still have
scrunched up in one pocket of a coat in a closet
kept in case I ever need it again.

THE DEATH OF PABLO NERUDA

On the 11th of September, *his wife said,*

there was no sign of illness. It was his custom
to be up for the early morning news and then
after breakfast to read through the newspapers
before beginning work. In France
some days before Pablo received the Nobel Prize
he was operated on for his prostate
and during surgery they discovered the tumor was malignant.
But though he never knew this—the doctors
asked me not to tell him—it was felt
the cancer was contained and operable and he would live
many years. His own doctor, Roberto Vargas Salazar,
said he would live at least six years and probably die
of something besides cancer, as his was well controlled.

On the 11th he watched TV and heard the radio bulletins
all day. It hit him very hard. The next day
he woke up with a fever. I called the doctor in Santiago
—we were living then at Isla Negra—and he
ordered some injections. But the nurse who was to give them
could not get through to us. She lived in a village
only five or six miles away, but the soldiers
would not let her pass for two days.

His fever did not diminish. We tried to call
friends in Santiago to find out what was happening
but they had already been arrested or gone into hiding.
The doctor had said on the phone not to let Pablo
hear what was happening, but he had a radio
right by his bed and heard everything they reported
including President Allende's last broadcast.
Salvador was a great friend of his; sometimes at Isla Negra
he would arrive unexpectedly: there would be a great noise
and it would be the president's helicopter descending.
He would stay for supper and they would talk. Salvador was
    planning
a big celebration for Pablo's 70th birthday next July
with guests invited from all over the world. Pablo

was working at this time on six books of poems,
     simultaneously,
and his memoirs, which his publisher in Buenos Aires
intended to bring out on his birthday.

On the 18th, some friends were able to reach the house
who told him what took place in Santiago.
This was very bad for him. He was very ill in the evening
and the next day I called an ambulance to take him
to the clinic in Santiago. Because of the trouble the police
     made
it took quite a while for the ambulance to get to us.
As we approached the city, we found the police
were checking everyone. I told them
this was Pablo Neruda in the ambulance, who is very ill.
They acted as though they had not heard me.
They made me leave his side and I was checked. This
affected him very much. When I got back in
I saw there were tears in his eyes: it was the first time
in my life I saw Pablo cry. I told him
not to make so much of it, they were checking
everybody. All this time
I did not think he was really badly off
but that it was mostly the fever, which he had had before.
But Pablo was broken inside.

When we got to the clinic, the place was almost deserted.
Pablo's doctor had been arrested, but we got
another doctor. I learned that my house in Santiago
had been attacked by the soldiers and burned:
this happened while the government was saying
they would protect Neruda's property. On the 20th,
the ambassador of Mexico came to the clinic
and told Pablo that the Mexican president, Luis Echeverría,
was sending a plane to take him there.
Pablo refused to go. We tried to convince him
that he had to leave, but he still said no.
We went outside the room, and the ambassador
told me I should tell him about the house.
We went back inside and I explained we could no longer stay.
At last he agreed to go. I left him to go back to Isla Negra

to get some of our possessions, returning on the 22nd.
I discovered that while I was away, despite a guard at the door,
some people had been in and told him what happened
to friends of his: all of this was very bad, Victor Jara,
one of his closest friends, was dead. Even our chauffeur,
who took no part in politics, was in jail
simply because he was our driver. That night

Pablo became delirious, crying out
"They are shooting them. They are shooting them."
I had the nurse give him an injection of tranquilizer
which I had in my purse. He slept
all night, and all the next day. At 10:30 at night
on the 23rd, while I was with him,
he had a convulsion and his heart stopped.
He passed from sleep to death; he did not suffer.

from
LIVING ON THE GROUND:
TOM WAYMAN COUNTRY
(1980)

WHAT GOOD POEMS ARE FOR

To sit on a shelf in the cabin across the lake
where the young man and the young woman
have come to live—there are only a few books
in this dwelling, and one of them
is this book of poems.

                              To be like plants
on a sunlit windowsill
of a city apartment—all the hours of care
that go into them, the tending and watering,
and yet to the casual eye they are just present
—a brief moment of enjoyment.
Only those who work on the plant
know how slowly it grows
and changes, almost dies from its own causes
or neglect, or how other plants
can be started from this one
and used elsewhere in the house
or given to friends.
But everyone notices the absence of plants
in a residence
even those who don't have plants themselves.

There is also (though this is more rare)
Bob Smith's story about the man in the bar up north,
a man in his 50s, taking a poem from a new book Bob showed
        him
around from table to table, reading it aloud
to each group of drinkers because, he kept saying,
the poem was about work he did, what he knew about,
written by somebody like himself.
But where could he take it
except from table to table, past the *Fuck offs*
and the *Hey, that's pretty goods*? Over the noise
of the jukebox and the bar's TV,
past the silence of the lake,
a person is speaking
in a world full of people talking.
Out of all that is said, these particular words

put down roots in someone's mind
so that he or she likes to have them here—
these words no one was paid to write
that live with us for a while
in a small container
on the ledge where the light enters

GARRISON

A man is running across Wyoming.
Away out on the high plains,
nothing around him but the wind and sky,
a man runs along the paved shoulder
of the great Interstate crossing Wyoming from west to east.
Cars pass him; the faces of children
stare out of rear windows.
And trucks pull by, the drivers high above the road
watch him run a long way ahead as they approach and go on.

Garrison is running across Wyoming.
He has always run. He ran in military school
and in the Army's summer camps.
"They wanted us to get up at 5:30 A.M.
So at 5 I'd be up doing laps. They couldn't believe it."
He went to college on a scholarship for track.
"I was good, but I wasn't that good.
I never could get into competition. I'd place,
but I think I only won in a meet once or twice.
I just liked to run. We'd have a good time,
me and a few others. I remember one relay
where the first guy on our team was great,
the second guy was good,
then they gave the baton to me.
I ran full out, but I lost most of the lead we had.
When I passed to my friend
he could see we weren't going to win:
he was even slower on that distance than I was.
So he ran one lap
then out of the stadium
into the dressing room
and was sitting outside having showered and changed
when the coach caught up to him.
The coach didn't know what to do.
He'd never seen anybody run right out of a race."

Now Garrison strides down a long hill in the afternoon sun,
his T-shirt plastered to his back, above the pavement,
face contorted with the strain.

"At college," he says,
"I used to run down from the jock dorm
about a mile to a little amusement park
where they had this miniature railroad
parents would take their kids on for rides.
There was a cinder track that paralleled the train tracks
so I'd run on that. Pretty soon
a train would come up behind
and I'd put on a burst of speed
to see if I could beat it.
The guy at the controls of the little engine
would open the throttle
nuh nuh nuh-nuh nuhnuhnuh and I'd tear ahead
trying to do better. People on board
would shout and wave
but I had to leap a couple of ditches
and in any case by the time I ever got to the park
I'd already run a ways so I wasn't exactly fresh.

"One day, though, I got into strip
and drove my car down.
I got out and hid in the bushes
on the further side of the worst ditch.
When the train came around the corner
I leaped out and yelled in the driver's ear
Let's go and took off up the track.
He opened her up *nuh nuh nuh-nuh nuhnuhnuh*
and took off after me, the people
screaming and cheering as he drew closer.
They thought they were helping win the race
but actually they were just sitting there yelling
and he would have gone faster if they weren't aboard.
Anyway, that time we were neck and neck
when we got round to the ditch again."

His feet, in Wyoming,
pull the asphalt behind him, stroke after stroke,
breath hauled in and pushed out with his long legs;
eyes blue under the blue sky.

He went to graduate school
in ROTC, studying education. He listened
to what people said about the War
and asked the Army about it,
so they let him go. After that,
he asked his professors about their work, too,
bringing his hound Ralph into classes
and offices, using the dog as a point of reference
in discussing teaching techniques.
He was living then at the edge of town
in a tiny cabin, and running
miles along the country roads
and laps around a tree-lined campus oval.

Until he quit, got a job working demolition,
⌐ ᴐn in the southern part of the state
went logging. "The only thing political down there,"
he says, "was the Birch Society meetings.
So I'd go along. Mostly it was a good place
to talk about hunting and trade guns and all that.
I'd refuse to take the oath of allegiance
to start the meeting. Freak 'em out.
Told them I was a Commie. Then we'd talk about dogs
and rifles. I kept winning most of the turkey shoots
they had down there, with my old single-shot.
They didn't know what to make of it. I figured
one crazy Commie at a Birch meeting
is better than a dozen films sent out from California.

"I remember one time I was over
talking guns with Billy Hankin.
I saw he had a couple of bumper stickers
on the back of his pickup:
Support Your Right To Bear Arms and
Support Your Local Police. 'Billy,' I said to him,
'you know if they pass a law outlawing guns
it isn't the Communists
who are going to come by to pick up your rifles.
It'll be Sheriff MacLeod.' Next time I saw the truck
the bumper sticker about the police was torn off."

He had enough education credits
to teach remedial subjects in the winters
and he logged, summers. He married
and got his teaching certificate finally,
had a daughter and hurt his back in the woods
so it had to be operated on.
Then his wife left him, and he came apart,
driving west to San Francisco non-stop
in his old jeep, and north into Canada
to a rural teaching job some friends got him.
There, too, he ran
and sat in the bar mourning his marriage
while the jukebox sang *you can't hide*
yer cheatin' eyes and he quit in January
and moved further north
to work as a counsellor on a ranch for delinquent boys.
"The kids could go to jail or to the ranch," he says.
"They were some mean little monsters.
A couple of them had been found guilty
of setting cars on fire. Shortly after they got to the ranch
they took off. We got the RCMP after them
and they were picked up in Hazelton.
The Mountie puts them into the back of his car
but one of them opens the door somehow
and zips away up the street. So the cop,
who isn't too bright, leaves one kid in the car
while he runs after the other.
By the time he gets back with the first kid,
sure enough, the other one had the cop car nicely ablaze.

"These kids are real puzzle-factory inmates,
penguins, that's what I call them. One night
a bunch of them got into a fight in the meal hall,
squirting ketchup at each other
and throwing bread around and everything.
I was supposed to be on duty, so I went in there
and didn't pay any attention to them
but began kicking over tables, smashing plates and cups,
tipping over chairs. Just went insane.
I looked up after a minute
and saw all the kids huddled into a corner

watching me. 'Now clean this up
and your mess too,' I said
and walked out, and they went to work
and got everything tidy. I just showed them
what it's like when an adult goes nutty.
No good yelling at them or threatening them.
They've had plenty of that.
If a penguin comes at me to hit me
sometimes I'll just wrap my arms around him
so he can't move his
and pick him up and dance with him. He gets really angry
but then he calms down and nobody gets hurt."

Now Garrison is travelling back to Colorado
for a long-delayed compensation hearing about his back.
"I never can do what I want to, Tom," he says
as we drive. "I got out of teaching because
I like to work with my hands. I have to stay in shape:
any job I've been on I want to work full out.
But most jobs, you're letting everybody else down
if you work too hard. I like the outdoor stuff at the ranch
but the place is crazy, it's really a jail,
the kids don't want to be there. And there's no women.
I go into town and meet somebody
and fall in love and make a fool of myself.
I don't want to do that. I want to be better to women.
But I don't know how."

His fingers reach up to twist
the thin blond hair above his forehead.
"Tom, who needs us? I mean
I think maybe this is the first time
people like us have been really useless.
What can we work at, give it everything
that isn't hurting someone else
or adding to the sick way things are going?
What are we good for? Sometimes I honestly wish
I'd gone and fought in the War."

At a rest-stop, he says he wants to stretch,
cramped from riding in the small car.

He changes into strip and starts east down the freeway
while I finish some lunch, check the oil
and drive out after him.
A speck in the distance
at the edge of the highway
Garrison runs as the traffic speeds past him
in the hot day. The only human figure
in the vast panorama
of wind and landscape, a man
is headed for Rawlins,
running across Wyoming,
running towards Jerusalem.

THE REFUGE

North of town, at dusk
we come out of Davidson's place and at the edge
of this clump of trees and cabins
named for the nearby waterfowl refuge
Burnett and Bobby Thompson build a huge stack of
branches and sawed-up pieces of trunk
from the dead elm the County had them cut down a week ago.

Burnett lights the pile. We sit to the east of it
under the old cottonwoods
and look out across the hayfield at the hills.

As the evening deepens, a thunderstorm
—flashes and rolls of sound—appears in the northwest:
the clouds moving out of the front range of the Rockies
and above the closer hogbacks, drifting east
toward the plains. A few drops
fall on us here and the fire
and Burnett
tosses another massive elm branch on the blaze
forcing a shower of sparks high into the night air.

Across the field, tiny lights of the farmhouse.
And further away, a few lights on the hills, dark
against the dark sky.
As the storm passes, the first stars.

Burnett and the others
begin considering how much hay
Farmer Glass can take off this field in a good season
and how he irrigates: still holding
pioneer water rights
as the land has remained in his family
since the first homesteading.
Burnett recalls working for Glass, getting the plow stuck
in a buffalo wallow near the lake: soil packed hard
where the beasts once rolled for pleasure, and Glass
yelling at him, showing him how to take the tractor through
and getting the plow stuck in the same place himself.

The talk
drifts into cattle: transfer fever
and other diseases, and their cure.

                                    A great moon
hangs in the southwest over the Refuge.
I sit in the darkness, breathing the smells of the hay
and the country, filled with a peaceful joy
at having driven so far to be with these friends again
here where so much has made me happy.

TRAVELLING COMPANIONS

At the bus station in Winnipeg
buying a ticket for Winkler, Manitoba,
Wayman hears a familiar voice behind him:
"Make that two to Winkler." Wayman turns, and
it's Four Letter Word.
"I told you to stay back at the hotel,"
Wayman says. "I'll only be gone for a day.
It's a high school reading
and they asked me specifically not to bring you."
"Nonsense," Four Letter word says,
reaching past Wayman to pay his portion of the fares.

"You're not welcome there," Wayman insists,
as he struggles out to the bus
with his suitcase and a big box of books to sell.
"That's not the point," Wayman's companion replies
as they hand their tickets to the driver
and climb up into the vehicle.
"Next you'll be ordered not to read
poems that mention smoking or drinking."

"I don't think you understand," Wayman begins
while the bus threads its way through the five o'clock traffic
and out onto the endless frozen prairie.
"The organizers of this program
asked me not to cause any trouble.
It seems somebody like you was brought into a school last year
and there were complaints all the way to the Minister of
        Education."

Four Letter Word stares out a window
at the darkening expanse of white snow.
"And you're the guy," he says at last,
"who's always telling people
I'm the one that gives the language its richness and vitality.
Didn't Wordsworth declare
poets should speak in the language of real men and women?"

"But it's a high school," Wayman tries to interject.
"Do you think the kids don't swear?" his friend asks.
"Or their parents? And I didn't want to bring this up,"
he continues, "but you depend on me. You use me for good
    reasons
and without me your performance will flop."
"No, it won't," Wayman says.
"It will," his companion asserts.
And the two ride through the deep winter night
in an unpleasant silence.

An hour later, they pull into the lights of Winkler
and here's the school librarian
waiting in the cold at the bus stop.
"You must be Wayman," he says
as Wayman steps down. "And is this a friend of yours?"
"I never saw him before in my life," Wayman responds
but his companion is already shaking hands with the librarian.
"So good to be here," he says, picking up Wayman's box of
    books.
"Now, when do we read?"

TEETHING

In the dark house, the cry of a child.
Her teeth are trying to be born:
the tiny incisors
are cutting their way up
through flesh, into a mouth
now open and crying.

Deep snow around the house
beside the forest. Indoors, in the night
the sleepy voice of the mother, then the father,
and the child's steady crying.
All at once the father is up, and a moment later
he brings the child into another room
and sits in an old rocker.

The noise of the chair starts
as its wooden dowels and slats
adjust repeatedly to the weight being swung
back and forth. The chair moves
not with the easy pace
of someone assured, experienced,
but with the urgent drive of a young man
rocking and rocking. The chair creaks
persistently, determinedly,
like the sound of boots on the snowy road outside
iun the day, going somewhere.

                        But it is here
the father has come to. In the dark room, in the chair
ten years as an adult pass, the chair
rocks out a decade of meetings, organizations, sit-ins.
It rocks out Chicago, and Cook County Jail.
It rocks out any means necessary
to end the War, fight racism, abolish the draft.
It rocks out grad school and marriage.
It rocks out Cambodia, and at last
jobs, a new country, and a child.

                                    But the chair
falls back each time
to the centre of things, so it also rocks back
all these lives up into these lives: the father
rocking
with his child in his arms
at the edge of sleep. In the still house at Salmon Arm
the sound of the rocking chair
in the winter night. Sudden cry of the child.
Cry of the world.

THE FEET

At night, the feet become lonely.

All day they have considerable importance:
are carefully dressed in shoes
and ready at any moment to stand,
move around, take the weight of the body.
When the body is sitting, sometimes
the feet depress certain pedals
to control an automobile travelling at tremendous speeds
for hundreds of miles.

But at night
even their socks are taken away.
The feet are made to lie down naked
in a part of the bed no one visits.
All night they lie there, with nothing to do.

Hidden away in the darkness
under sheets and blankets,
no wonder the two abandoned feet
begin a clumsy relationship.
One foot
suddenly crosses the ankle of the other
like a blind horse putting his head over the neck of another
        blind horse.
The feet lie like this for hours
—stiff, self-conscious, not making a sound.

LA LLUVIA DE TU MUERTE

He died on a rainy Tuesday in the autumn
and the rain washed him away.

He died in Vancouver, our City, in the morning
and the rain washed him away.

The rain washed away his face, the face of a brother.
The rain washed away what a face feels
as the drops of rain strike it
on a street, in Vancouver,
and the rain washed him away.

It took his name, the name of my friend,
and left only the letters of his name.
It took the way he walked
and what he did Saturday afternoons.
It took art galleries, used furniture stores, libraries;
it took Kitsilano Beach.
It took everything he ever saw
and it washed him away.

He died with thunder in his mind:
thunder without sound
but with each flash of lightning so white and sudden
his ears rang continually.
He died of cancer, which in thirty years
may be as preventable as polio is now.
But in this time, in these thirty years, cancer killed him at
    thirty.

After thirty, men's faces begin to fatten.
After thirty, it begins to be obvious
many people will never amount to much.
After thirty is late to marry, late to begin a family.
Even so, he died at thirty
and the rain washed him away.

When a great pain fills the body
what you are leaves

so all that remains of you is the shell of the pain
and an enormous fear.
He died in pain.
But he lived in a quick wit, intricate, subtle,
and what he thought he passed on to those around him.
Like every friend, he taught me, and like no other
this one taught me some ways to think about writing, about
    art.
He taught some people about rain, but not me.
He died in the rain.

He died in the rain and the world got smaller
for me, because when he was alive he was a brother
and when he died, a brother.
He was alive, and he died, and there is still the struggle.
And a shadow where he was, and the rain.

from
COUNTING THE HOURS:
CITY POEMS
(1983)

ASPHALT HOURS, ASPHALT AIR

for Ron Baxter and Bron Wallace

Men are as mature
as the forces of production
of their times allow them to be.

—T.W. Adorno

1. Quitting In The Spring

Windsor, eight a.m.; the shifts already begun.
In the light rain, a man eating breakfast in his car
on the Kentucky Fried Chicken lot: the revolving sign
broken, fluorescent tubes
visible through the missing plastic.

Curbside trees
keep some of the sidewalk dry.
Groups of children are headed for school
carrying books and umbrellas.
A girl driving a small car
stops for another girl
who gets in, smiling.

"At the plant, this guy in his late fifties
has a bench alongside the tool crib
for his chests of spare parts: the repairman.
If something is broken on a drill
or a fitting gone on an air hose,
we usually say, 'Throw it out.' But he
will carefully manufacture small copper washers
to fix the routers, and take all morning
to loosen a hand jigsaw we can't get to budge.
Inside the lid of one of his chests
is a row of ticket stubs
to the Union's Christmas party
for the past sixteen years. In the midst of all the bustle,
somehow he has gotten a corner
to work away at things at his own pace."

151

"When I went back after a year
the foreman says—he was taking me around
in a bunch of new-hires—he says to me:
'We'll put you over here, son, to start.
It's not too difficult.'
'That's good,' I told him,
'because I'm *real* dumb,
and I work *real* slow.'
He looked at me for a second:
'You've worked here before,' he says."

"Once I decide I'm going to quit
it's like doing hard time in jail:
I know I shouldn't
but I count down.
The last job I had, warehousing,
I was going to quit in the Spring
but then decided to stay on through August
and finally gave my notice
for the end of September.
I guess everybody does it a little—
some guys always have it figured
how many weeks until their vacations,
and the crew by the small parts spray booth
put up a sign each December:
'Only 14 working days until Christmas.'
But with me, once I know I'm going
I can tell you how many more *minutes*
I have left to work."

In the small grocery store on Wyandotte
after school hours or on weekends
the son or daughter are at the cash register:
both in their teens, bored and sullen,
throwing the customers' purchases into the bags,
while their grandfather
sits on a soft drink crate behind them
reading his newspaper.

"Occasionally when it rains
I'll be up at Final Assembly fixing parts short

and I feel the cold air
coming in despite the heaters.
I look through the doors,
and for a few minutes
I'm happy to be inside, working."

"Somebody stuck an announcement
on the Union bulletin board
attacking the executive for calling a second vote
on the dues increase. One of the stewards
saw it and tore it up. I was speaking to Arnie
and said I thought what the steward did wasn't right.
Arnie says: 'No. That note was out of line.
I'm against the increase, too,
but these things should be argued
at a Union meeting, not in front of the Company.'
Larry leans over and says:
'You talk, Arnie,
as if there's two opposite sides here.'"

On Sundays, the bells of the churches:
sounds of another trade,
like the horns of the boats in Fleming Channel
bound downriver with iron ore or coal
for Ford Rouge. So many cars
with a small group of effigies on the dashboard
or the rear window shelf:
Mary, in blue and white plastic,
surrounded by plastic roses.

"Earle, the new guy, is telling us
his wife is nineteen.
'I'm glad she don't know
what we do all day,' he says.
'When I come home at night
I tell her how worn out I am
and she lets me just sit
while she gets supper.
If she knew what this job was like
she'd probably want me to help, too.'
'That's something I've wondered about,'

153

Brian says. 'Nothing we lift is that heavy
and we got the winches if it is.
Why don't they hire women?
It'd sure make this place more enjoyable.'
And Earle says: 'No *way*.
This is a *man*'s job.'"

At lunch, by the parts desk:
"A fellow I know came home from work last week
and found his wife gone.
She took almost everything.
She only left one knife, one fork, one spoon
—like that—one plate, one cup."
And somebody else adds:
"It happened to a friend of mine, too.
And when he went into the bedroom
all his clothes were on the floor:
she left him one coat hanger."

The rain falling steadily on the pavement.

And Jim's story, about staying up Thursday night,
stoned, and punching in at work late
after just a few hours sleep.
The foreman has him in the metal shop
where the truck bodies are assembled and spot welded.
At the first break, someone remarks
how for a change that morning
none of the machines had broken down
and they hadn't been any parts short.
At this rate, the guy points out,
if nothing else went wrong they could make production
by two o'clock.
"For the next couple of hours," Jim says,
"we kept working as fast as we could.
By lunch we had trucks on every hook of the line
across most of the department. And afterwards
we went even faster. Everybody in our area
got into it: not just the longhairs
but even the immigrants and the lifers.
A couple of the guys are yelling:

Trucks. More trucks. Build more trucks.
And we're all hustling like crazy.
The foremen began to be nervous
because there was nothing for them to do.
Get out of the way, people were joking with them:
Who needs you? Go have a coffee
and come back Monday.
Then something weird happened: the foremen
start pushing the trucks *back*,
trying to slow the work down.
This was so out of character
everybody cracked up.
Hey, what are you assholes doing?
people were shouting and laughing:
Why don't you just go home?
After the last break, though,
we returned to our usual speed
and finished only half an hour early.
But it was such fun there for a while,
at the end of the day
I didn't even feel very tired."

2. What The Women Said

"When I told my parents
I was going to leave him
my father became enraged,
yelling out: *Whore.*
He dragged me to the window
and pointed down the street toward the jail.
That's where you're going to end up,
he shouted at me, *there*
or in the nut house. I looked at
my mother, but she left the room."

"Well, we eat at that place
because he likes Harvey's
better than McDonald's.
Depending on how hungry he is:
McDonald's when he says he's really starved."

"Working for them
is sort of a family thing.
Those of us in the office, a lot of our husbands
are out on the trucks.
The Company likes it that way
but it isn't always so good:
we work a regular eight-thirty to four-thirty
but the guys work all different shifts.
If they get off before us, sometimes they'll go drinking
and won't get home until the bar closes.
On other shifts, they're asleep all day
and when we get home they've gone to work.
We only get to see each other at breakfast."

    "He came up behind
    as she was crossing the parking lot by the church
    with her arms full of groceries.
    He got her around the neck
    so she dropped the bags,
    and he held a knife in front of her
    and told her he'd kill her,
    he'd kill her if she said anything.
    All this time he was pulling her backwards
    under the shadows of the trees.
    He got her to sit, and knelt with her.
    He kept jabbing the knife at her throat
    while he pawed at her with his other hand,
    exciting himself.

        "All at once she tried
    to catch hold of the knife, and he hit her
    with his other hand, hard, in the stomach.
    Then he pulled at her belt, and her jeans,
    and she said she felt lost
    like when your bladder let you down one day at school
    or you couldn't run home fast enough.
    But she started to scream
    and the man took off."

"The day after we won the arbitration
and were going to get the same rate as the men,

the foreman announces
we're being transferred to another department
where—guess what?—we'll be paid at the old rate.
We sat down, refused to work,
and everything in our area came to a halt.
During the next hour or so
women and men from all over the plant
stopped by to tell us if the Company tried to fire us
or go through with the transfer
they'd walk out. But then the foreman
shows up with someone from the Union, and *he* insists
the Company has the right."

"Bruce tells me he thinks about it:
at the office, sooner or later
he works with a woman he likes, who likes him.
But he realizes, with me and the kids,
he'd be risking more than he gains.
He tries to be humorous, he says:
let her know about his attraction for her
but turn it into something they can laugh at
and so keep working together."

"My Dad, when I was fourteen,
used to put his hand down my pants all the time
and my uncle would laugh—
it was supposed to be a joke.
But I'd cry, and my mother told me:
Don't say anything to anybody; he's your father
and my uncle would, too, and my father would tell me:
If this gets beyond this house,
you're really in trouble."

"It wasn't till years later
when I thought about that first time
I realized what it was: I told him, *No*,
but he was stronger
and we *had* been going out.
I did like him a little, but
not enough to do that,

157

and I told him so, but he did, and
that was the first."

"I asked him
to touch me there,
and he said: 'What's the matter?
My cock not good enough for you?'"

"Anna says she has to clean
and cook for her husband, their two kids,
her cousin who boards with them—he pays
$150 a month, meals and lodging—
and herself. Everything has to be kept clean,
she says, so as well as the laundry
and the daily dishes and the floors,
 she says she does the walls every week
and the ceiling every other week.
All this plus the shopping and cooking,
and some mending, and she has a job two nights a week
selling popcorn and candy at a local theater.
It's about eight hours a week, at the minimum wage,
but it all helps. Just once, she says,
she told her husband she was going on strike.
When he got home from work
she was over at a neighbor's:
the breakfast dishes hadn't been done,
the house was a mess
and she didn't have supper ready.
He was furious, and came over and got her.
'I told you I was going on strike,'
she says, but he was really angry:
'He told me he'd really let me have it
if I ever did it again.' She's twenty-four."

"They got no kids
and he doesn't want her to work
so she's alone all day, and
does sewing and stuff around the house.
She tries to please, but whatever he wants
is what *she* wants, so when he asks her,
she says: "What do *you* think?"

And he gets mad: 'Don't you have a mind?'
he says."

"My brother is at home
because he got hit
by a boxcar in the yards—he works as a brakeman.
So he's relaxing
and telling everyone
how dangerous his job is.
Then I quit
because the boss is after me all the time.
'I can make things easy for you,'
he says. 'You ought to be nice to me.'
He's always grabbing me, and when I tell him
to take his hands off,
he gets mean, then the next day
starts being nice again.
It's just crazy so I left.
Now I can't get U.I. for weeks
because they say I left without a good reason.
And I'm home too,
but I don't get Compensation for what happened to me.
I can't even use that place as a reference
to find another job."

3. Dieppe Park

How does this change?
We who construct the City every day:
what keeps us crawling over each other
in the dark
in different directions,
certain we are going some place better?

October 14, 1976: three hundred of us wait
in Dieppe Park, here to honor the day of protest
the unions have called against the government controls
that hold our wages steady while prices rise.
Behind the speakers' platform, the Detroit River,
and on the far side of that another country:
the skyscrapers of downtown Detroit.

Finally, the spokesmen appear on stage
and Ron says to me: "Look. It's the living dead."
An old man begins to talk about the great strikes
a quarter-century ago, when all the auto plants were out
and in one action Riverside Drive was clogged with strikers'
        cars
—that strike won by the Union at last
with the birth of the Rand Formula.
But the crowd this morning is bored—mostly young people
impatient to march in the cold air, knowing the unions now
as something else: the activists isolated and removed
or bought off with jobs in the hierarchy;
the union protection and grievance systems
all that stands between the bosses and ourselves,
but the bureaucracy uncaring and slow
so that often only our own actions
—stoppages on the line, or walkouts,
or the threat of these—bring issues to a quick solution.
Even today, this is not a strike the unions have called
to continue until we win,
but a day off work, with tomorrow
to be the same as yesterday.

Before the last speaker is finished
we begin to move toward the road.
Dozens of union marshals are ready, however,
to ensure the march travels at a fast pace
up Ouellette and round by City Hall
and then dissolves—as though the organizers
are anxious to get this over with.

Yet there is a strike on here
against a department store chain
refusing union recognition in one of their suburban stores.
The Company has held out for months:
hundreds of people each Saturday
stream in past the pickets, to be waited on inside
by other citizens who daily cross these lines to work.
This far from the beginnings of unions,
it is as though we have to start over:
but now when someone explains

that without the founding of these organizations
we would all still work for subsistence wages,
at the whim of every company foreman—
for intolerable hours, with safety, Compensation,
unemployment payments and pensions
nonexistent, or worse than they are—
those whom we speak to
can point to corruption, meanness, bullying
and use these as their excuse
to cross our lines. This October day
in the crowd being hurried up the main street,
somebody suggests we march
through the downtown branch of the store.
The idea spreads with shouts, but the marshals
are quick to stop it: a group of them
take up positions in the street in front of the store's entrance
to say: *Keep moving. Keep moving.*

And at the Park, a middle-aged man
stood at the microphone for the Social Democrats.
He informs us he is our representative
in the provincial parliament, and if we re-elect him
and more like him
all will be well with us.

                                But he is nervous
as if he senses from this crowd's listless response
something here can tell he is lying.
A couple of young men not far from me
begin to heckle, and I ask myself
why do I also feel such anger?
This man is not a boss, not an owner.
Yet I do not expect
the parties of the rich to understand
what this life is like, why it has to be altered,
but this man and his party know
and they do nothing. Out of office, they talk,
and when they have been elected
they behave almost exactly
as the parties they say they oppose. They declare
they are the only alternative, they put forward a vision,

but in power, they cannot implement these things,
they explain, because the time isn't right.
"We will win more votes in the long run," they say,
"if we legislate you back to work,
if we do not institute the day care we promised.
Then, in the long run, you'll benefit
even if you lose again now."

Perhaps I loathe them
because they are that part of ourselves
that keeps us children, looking to someone other than
        ourselves,
bigger than ourselves, to redeem us.
This man, and the men and women like him,
see how we live
and plan to use this to get more for themselves.

And yet when we turn to each other,
many times we recognize only the powerless
and lash out: what we offer ourselves
is a human fist
smashing into a human face
—male or female—a tiny model
of what our days feel like.

                    Later this year
an unemployed auto worker with a grievance,
getting no help from the Windsor Union office,
went out to his car and returned
with a rifle, shooting, so that the staff
dived under desks or tables, or fled
to hide in washrooms and closets.
Then the man left; the rooms and hallways
suddenly quiet. But he went outside
around the building
and peered in through the windows of the executive offices
and saw Charlie Brooks under his desk
and fired through the glass and killed him.
And though what Brooks was head of
is one more organization that claims to be ours,
to speak for us, and yet so often blocks us,

at the moment Brooks was given those bullets
he was not the minister responsible for unemployment
        insurance,
he did not own GM.

4. Why There Is No Calm Here

Day and night, the huge blue trucks
of Chrysler's, and the others
climb the great iron bridge from both directions
constantly pulling
the sound across the river:
Detroit-Windsor, Windsor-Detroit.

Like the clouds
headed south out of Michigan
the trucks and trailers
travel high in the air between the cities.
But the wheels and engines
pulse at my ear, while the clouds

drift into Ontario in perfect silence.

5. Recording Tachometer

Something more
needs to be said in our lives.
At the Union local meeting
called right after work for once, the business agent
looks out at our faces and asks
if anyone has any complaints.
And nobody says a word,
but we sit heavily in the chairs
of the rented dance hall, until one man rises
and speaks about his steward, in Rigid Frame
where the trucks too large for the line are built.
He reports how the steward is dangerous to work with,
disregarding safety rules together with the foreman,
so that even the plant Safety Committee has spoken to him
yet it continues to happen. And the business agent says:

Well, you elected him. It's your problem.
Any other difficulties?

But as well as this grievance
there is the grievance of the faces:
expressed not in words
but by the young, energetic,
tossing washers at each other
all day in the plant—or, in the office,
elastic bands. And by Archie, older than the rest of the crew,
refusing to work in the area
when the vacuum attachment to the fibreglass cutter
breaks again, flooding the air here with
thousands of tiny floating particles of glass.
And Dave telling the young partsman: "Get a ladder.
Don't climb up the racks hand over hand."
And the guys on engine assembly nearby saying:
"Yeah. Slow down.
Don't you know there's an energy crisis?"

Yet despite the arguments with the foremen,
and the general foreman, the wildcats, the strikes,
though so many units are lost to production
or we quit,
in the end we go back
to these hours here
at the machines—which while they transform
time and materials
also do something to us.

We must begin to ask
about another life, the life we feel in the ads
for charter holidays, in the ads for clothing, stereos,
lotteries, our own cars. What happens to us
growing up, so that Bill, forty-five years old,
seeing the foreman approaching one day
when we've stopped work for a moment to talk to each other,
shouts: *Look out. Here comes the teacher.*

Someone is stealing our time, our time alive,
and all our lives are marked by that theft.

They have told us that time is money
and since money can be owned
you can possess a man or a woman's time
and spend the human beings who live in that time
like a coin or a dollar. In some trucks
we are ordered to install
a recording tachometer, so that the owners
can constantly check
on the driver: the device tells how the driver shifts,
when he stops the vehicle, how fast he was driving
at any time. So even the man alone on the highway
has the foreman watching—he remains in the factory,
like the man or woman in the bar after supper
with one eye on the clock because even off work
somebody owns your time.

                              Of course they insist
this is the only possible arrangement
whereby things can get built, the City function.
But who stands to say: *This is not good enough?*

Out of the skill and thought
we apply on the job every day
—learning how to compensate for a particular machine
to get it to produce what it is supposed to
or what we want from it—
and from our craft and decisions
which they tell us are of no particular importance
since each hour that passes is worth precisely the same
like the numbers spinning on the dials of a gasoline pump,
out of our combined accomplishments
and ideas, the change in our daily life must come.

And it is ourselves
who will have to define it and fight for it.
But it is a life
we cannot live alone: while a woman is afraid
to walk home at night, while a man or woman is desperate
for comfort or food, this time and place we share
is made worse. Out of all our imperfections,

fears, distrust, we must for our own lives
stand together against the owners of our time.

Little will improve
without this daily understanding
we have to release time itself
from its buyers and sellers.
For time, like the air,
is indivisible: where one of us is chained in time,
or has our time locked away from us,
time itself is injured—the same time
we have to live in. We have a book that says
on the seventh day a god freed time a little.
And there is our history in which we know
the struggle for eight hours won a little more.
But as long as there are wages—
so that we must obtain what we need to live
and live ourselves
according to how many pieces can be made in a day
or according to the money some hours of the day are worth—
time is still jailed, and that is the factory
we are all in.

Saturday, the Windsor air
reverberates with the noise of muscle cars, vans, pickups.
This May, in the garages by the back lanes,
snowmobiles wait for another winter of motors.

But on Monday, the high-performance cars
will be motionless
in the parking lots of the plants.
They will be silent
later today in front of the houses and apartments
where someone else goes on working at home.
In these hours, though,
the weekend tires and engines
power around town.
And all afternoon
the streets fill
with the horns of weddings.

THE DETROIT STATE POEMS: TENNENHOUSE

A rainy morning in Detroit
and the roof of State Hall
is leaking water again into the fourth floor.
Pools form under one of the skylights
and buckets have been placed out
in the corridors. A secretary
is checking each faculty office,
making a list of those of us flooded out:
two doors along, somebody is working at his desk
wearing rubber boots; his swivel chair
rolls through an inch of water
as he wheels back to answer the phone.

                            Money
is what the university lacks: the interior walls scarred
and dirty, like any factory, the daily office garbage here
emptied only twice a week, repairs
taking months to be attended to.

Tennenhouse sticks his head in
on his way back from an early class:

"Did I tell you, Tom, my family
originally settled near Winnipeg
when they first came from Europe?
They homesteaded, but they knew nothing
about farming; it was one of the sons who finally realized
the land they had chosen was worthless,
after years of trying. A few of my relatives
are still there, but my father
and some others moved to Detroit:
they were either going to use farm machinery
or make it. We'd have these gatherings
where the farming uncles would talk
to the auto plant uncles. The farm ones would tell about
killer hailstorms
that suddenly come up: a whole year's crop
and work ruined in a second, the stones
big enough to kill cattle

and, if you were caught in the open,
people. And the auto shop uncles
tell how sometimes a car at the end of the line
being tested will explode:
sending a hail of metal
through that part of the plant
—which is even more deadly.

"It always impressed me; it's the same
image," Tennenhouse says,
"doing either job. I guess I'm the only one of the family so far
who's really made it in out of the rain."

And he walks on down the hallway to his door
with his pipe and his books
skirting the standing water on the linoleum
and the slow drops being caught by the pails.

THE DETROIT STATE POEMS: MARKING

I begin each essay with a calm mind—
a fresh start.
But as I consider what they have written
I get angry: the most cursory of rereadings
would have caught this sentence fragment,
and here is a misused semicolon
after we spent more than an hour on that in class
and where I talked to this student individually
for another thirty minutes about this persistent mistake.
And instead of the simple structure of the expository paper
which we have also gone over and over
and which can be so helpful a model, a technique, a guide,
here again is a jumbled series of random observations:
trite, contradictory, obviously hurried
and spelled wrong.

My red pencil becomes enraged.
It stalks through the words,
precise, bitter, vindictive,
acting as if it is pleased to discover error
and pounce on it, hacking and destroying and rearranging,
furiously rooting out sloppiness and weakness
as though upholding some stern moral precept
against another, softer age.

But the hand gripping the pencil
begins to tremble with remorse.
It feels it has led the students on
to try to express themselves
and then betrayed them:
attacking what they have exposed
of their ideas and emotions.
What use is righteousness, the hand wishes to ask the pencil,
without charity?

I read the name at the top
and think of the young person whose effort this is.
Now all I see on the paper
is a face, crestfallen when I hand back what they attempted.

Eyes look up at me
apprehensively, as at a judge.
We both know my weighing of their skill
will be taken to be an assessment of themselves.

It is as though I have been asked to mark
not essays but their faces,
not sentences but who they are.
I raise my pencil, but my hand still shakes.
I want to show them what in normal English usage
is considered incorrect.
But I can not assign a grade to their eyes.

TWO STUDENTS LOOKING AT A POSTCARD OF A PAINTING BY GUSTAV KLIMT WHILE LISTENING TO GAVIN WALKER PLAY JAZZ AT THE CLASSICAL JOINT COFFEE HOUSE, VANCOUVER, B.C.

Drums again along the inlet:
two blocks south of the docks
on a rainy Thursday evening,
white man's drums
filling the room with a white rain.
At a table a young man and a young woman
here on a date begin the first touches and whispers
that will lead to another beginning with the flesh.
But now she holds onto his sweater at his chest
as she leans to put her mouth at his ear
to say something through the music.
He is the more shy of the pair.
Yet his arm touches her sweatered arm
as he bends his head almost into her hair to reply.
Her fingers stay on his shoulder;
his face is dazed with pleasure and fear.

Now Gavin Walker rises to the microphone
with his alto sax, and begins.
He is less than a meter from the two
crowded in at a front table, but the young man
sits partly turned from the music
staring down at his coffee, while the woman
watches the musicians past his face.
Gavin Walker strains at his work, his right foot
lifts from the floor
as his saxophone throws
into the steady falling white water of the drums
the notes that are harsh sparks
of reddish-brown light. At his back
the two others of his group
half-interestedly follow him: the electric bass
placing its bars of black sound
underneath the others' music, and the electric guitar
releasing from time to time into the room
its clusters of floating yellow globes.

At the table in front, the young man turns
and from the chairback pulls out of an inside pocket of his coat
a postcard of a painting by Gustav Klimt.
He lays the card flat on the table, positioned
so the young woman can see
and she bends her head to look at it too,
their hair almost touching.
It is a glittering pattern of gold and muted colors
meant to depict a woman. They do not speak.
After a few seconds
the young man takes the card from the table
and returns it to his coat again.

But now he sits with his back to her, facing the musicians.
The young woman rests her chin gently on his shoulder,
her arm around his body, holding him.
Gavin Walker finishes a solo run, but no one claps;
the drums and electric strings
drive the music forward through the night.

Before the set is over, the young man and young woman
get up to go. Gavin Walker is working again;
they have to squeeze between the microphone and the table
in order to leave. They move past him in their coats
into the wet darkness outside the door
carrying the postcard with them.

Gavin Walker does not watch them go.
It is almost midnight. He will do a slow ballad next
and then an old Miles Davis piece. After the break
he will cut the second set off short.
There are always smaller crowds on a rainy night
and this evening hardly anyone will be left in the room to hear.

NEW AND USED

after "Don Asterio Alarcón"

It's a port all right,
Vancouver, with the wind
from the harbor docks
blowing along Hastings Street
where the bottles wash up
in front of beer parlors
and short-time hotels
and paper of all kinds
drifts, and out-of-town
loggers and
sailors and miners
and the citizens
busy with their urban trades
and the police.

But a block away
at the top of Victory Park
where the men and women
sleep on the grass
is a street of
booksellers.

Here a dusty store
keeps a rack of ten-cent volumes
out by the bus stop
the way a skid-road grocery
puts spoiled broccoli and cauliflower
outside for quick sale. And two doors down
is the Party's bookshop
with news from Moscow and
Cuba and across the road
the Anglicans
sell their greeting cards and tracts.
And then at the corner
MacLeod's Books—
New and Used.

Inside, at the rear
of the dim room of floor-to-ceiling books
a man leans on a counter and stares
through to the windows in front.
And whoever old MacLeod was
and what he was like
this isn't him but the present owner
young Donald Stewart.
For all business like this
contain time and sell time
almost without noticing it
so one day in the quiet
MacLeod wasn't there
and Don Stewart was.

And person by person
the City stops in to see him
as they did the old man:
this one is looking
for dictionaries, and this one
for recipes, and this man
wants novels by
a certain Argentine
(in translation of course)
and here somebody
is examining the maritime section
while another peers at
Chinese history
or a few feet on railroads.

And since books
go around like money
others drop by to offer Don Stewart
school texts, or
science fiction, lurid confessions
and manuals on how to sew.
Thieves try to sell him
lavish art books
and a few orders of new editions
arrive by mail.
And always the poets appear

with their insistent
collections.

And Don Stewart
sorts through these volumes
patiently filling the holes
a day's sales make in his shelves.
He stands at the back by the cash register
like old MacLeod probably
in jeans and a gray sweater that shows
a green shirt at one elbow.

Years pass
in this shop
in silence
and a turning of pages
and Don Stewart
goes on with each day like anyone
to whom time is only
a deepening of value:
rare books becoming rarer
while the others change hands.

So when Time himself
with his scythe and hourglass
opens the door and steps in
Don Stewart will watch him
without fear or regret.
For Time is at home here
browsing among the stock.
And when he gets to the back
with a few volumes under his arm
he always meant to buy,
Don Stewart, grown old now,
will ring up his last sale
just as usual
and then the two
past the astonished customers
will go out together
talking of books.

TAKING THE DEAD OUT OF MY ADDRESS BOOK

Jeff Marvin

In the cold days before the New Year
I am taking the dead out of my address book.

I pass a line through the names.
Some were the parents of friends,
one was buried deep in the earth,
another burned in the air.
Now word has come of one
caught between the sky and the ground,
frozen far down a crevice,
suspended, too difficult to hook
and pull up.

While this happened
my address book went on carrying them
like a tree that keeps its dead leaves
hung as dusty rags
all winter.

When I get a new book
there will be no trace on its pages
that these people lived
—like lovers or friends
who after years we never see.
My name
meantime is written and vanishes
in other people's pages, too,
rehearsing the moment
it will disappear
forever.

At the printers,
men and women watch the machines
turn out sheets of ruled paper,
ready to be trimmed and bound,
to hold names.

And further off is a mountain
covered with white snow.

MEETING NEEDS

Man makes his history not in order to march along
a line of predetermined progress, and not because
he must obey the laws of some abstract . . .
evolution.
    He does so in the endeavor to satisfy his own needs.

—G.V. Plekhanov,
The Materialist Conception of History

I walk into the Waldorf bar on Hastings one evening
in case Mark, or anybody I know, is here
and at a couple of tables pushed together
a group of men and women appear familiar.
"Wayman," one of the men calls,
waving me over,
but I can't place where I've seen him before.
"Sit down, sit down," he says enthusiastically.
"We were just talking about you."

As I sit, somebody puts a beer in front of me
and I fumble to add my money to the pile.
"We figured you'd be down tonight,"
the man continues, and around the tables
other heads nod agreement.
"It's, uh, great to see you," I say,
taking a sip of my beer. "But—
where do I know you from?"
"Don't you recognize us?" asks a voice from the other table
and I realize everyone is staring at me now.
"We're your needs."

                    "My needs?" I say,
putting down my beer glass. There are about ten of them,
young, casually dressed, as though just off work.
Of the two women present, I can't help observing
how beautiful one is, and to my surprise
she smiles back.

"Certainly,"
the man who first spoke to me says.
"I'm Friendship. This pig beside me,"
he gestures to a portly young man in a windbreaker
with his mouth full of potato chips, "is Food."
"You really don't remember us?" the young man on my left
        breaks in
and I notice he has a carpenter's apron, hammer, and hard
        hat
on the floor by his chair. "That's Shelter,"
Friendship resumes, "and the dude past him in the fancy
        cowboy shirt
is Clothing."

                "Pleased to meet you,"
I say, extending my hand. "We first met when you were a
        baby,"
Clothing says as we shake,
"but you probably don't recall that."
"No," I say, and Friendship goes on with the introductions.
By now I can grasp what's happening,
and assume accurately that the one half-slumped
at the other end of the table is Drink
and wait impatiently for Friendship to get around
to the particularly lovely woman, who, sure enough,
smiles invitingly at me once more.
When Friendship finishes, I try to broach a delicate question.
"If you're my needs," I inquire,
"shouldn't there be someone here named, uh,
New Stereo?" "Only you can answer that,"
Friendship says, looking at me intently:
"We're your needs, not your wants."
While I'm considering this,
Food stands up
and asks if anyone would like more beer nuts or anything.
"Naw, but get us another round,"
Drink requests, and I turn to Friendship again.
"There's somebody missing who I think *is* a need of mine,"
I say: "Where's Major Social Change?"
"The Major?" Shelter responds. "She's . . .
sort of different." "She?" I ask.

179

"Yeah," two or three people confirm.
"But he's, that is, she's a need we all have," I insist.
"Isn't she one of you?"

                             "Not exactly,"
the beautiful woman down the table says.
"But couldn't we be doing a lot better?" I ask her.
"Shouldn't there be more of you here?
Where's Employment, for instance?"
"He ain't talking to you right now,"
Art, the other woman present, answers.
"You're telling *me*," I begin,
but we pause for a moment while a waiter
unloads two fresh beer for each of us
and Food returns with a half-dozen packages
of nuts and chips for each table.
"If Employment were here," I resume,
"I have a few thousand complaints
to speak to him about."

                         "He claims you don't like him,"
Friendship says. "The way things are," I explain,
"I don't like what he does when I'm with him
and I don't like what he does to my friends.
I know he's only a reflection of the system we live under . . ."
"Actually, it's the other way around,"
interrupts a small guy with glasses sitting opposite me
I hadn't noticed before.

                      "Okay," I agree, "but my point is
he's not going to improve without Major Social Change.
In fact, without her,
none of you are going to alter much for the better.
Not that you're not adequate now,"
I add hastily, as everyone starts to frown,
"or I guess you wouldn't be here.
But there are others absent too.
Who's responsible for me having a real voice
in what happens to my neighborhood, or the City, or . . .?"
"You mean Self-Determination," Friendship says.
"Whatever he's called," I say.

                              "She,"
someone corrects from along the table.
"She," I say. "But I'd like her
to be together with Employment."
"She'd put him through some changes,"
Art nods. "Plus," I say,
"there are those of you who haven't met people I know
in quite a while, or who offer a pretty meager appearance
when you do arrive."
"I'm aware of that," Friendship says.
"And what about me needing to feel confident
some of you aren't going to give me the brush-off
in a month or so?" I go on. "You're talking about Security,"
Shelter says. "Exactly," I say, "which is yet another reason
I'd expect Major Social Change to be with you."

"You've misunderstood something," the little guy with glasses
breaks in again. "The Major always declares her role
is to help us get together with people.
But she maintains when she spent time with us in the past
it didn't work out very well."
"She says something about
a confusion
between means and ends," Shelter says.
"We've been close for years," the little guy resumes,
"but she really isn't one of us.
For example," he continues,
"you'll never find her down here."

"That's her loss," Drink says,
as he beckons the waiter.
And we order the same again all around.

WHITE HAND

The chain saw bites into the wood: the faller
is making the undercut
then his back cut.
And when the tree is felled
it is bucked to length,
and later the rigging crew
hauls it out to a landing.
Danger is everywhere: the rotten tops
of snags, or when a cable unexpectedly tightens
or parts, or a log slips from the grapple
and rolls. Shadowed by death, the log is carried by truck
and then perhaps to the world
of water, boomsticks and swifters
and tugs, and on to the mills.

But in the green brush
two hands stay on the chain saw
for months.
The chain cuts into the wood, the heavy saw
is lfited in, jams, is worked free
and lifted into the cut again,
for years. The constant motion
of the engine, the chain,
is sawing too
at the smallest of blood vessels
and nerves: as in the guts of a cat operator,
what in the hand of this man
is shaking free
cannot grow back—white hand,
they call it, the hand gone permanently numb,
useless . . .

I take a sheet of paper
and place its sharp corners
in my typewriter roller and turn it,
and around the roller, facing my keys,
appears first the tip
of a man's middle finger, then the tops
of the others, so I type the poem

on the palm of a man's hand, a brother's:
white page
white hand

from
THE FACE OF JACK MUNRO
(1986)

ARTICULATING WEST

In May
I shook the prairie dust
out from under my tires
and took the route
over the Kicking Horse
and Rogers Pass,
meeting wet snow once
that day high in the forest,
and once hail,
until, descending,
at
Revelstoke
I ran into green:
the twelve different shades of green
and of yellow
in the springtime woods—
alder trees, the ferns and underbrush
and even fresh green
on the tips of the evergreen spruce.
And I rolled down the highway
filling my lungs with
the good green air, until near Sicamous
I turned off to follow the Shuswap River
deeper into the green: along that road
the lilac was in violet blossom
and the apple in white blossom
and each green farm
tucked in among the green hills
had its small orchard
of peaches or cherries.
And the green interior
of my green car
began to sprout: little woody shoots
appeared on the dashboard
and winding out of the handbrake handle,
tendrils and stalks and unfolding leaves
poking out of the glove compartment
and around the edges of the floor mats.
The steering wheel in my fingers

started to have the feel of fibre
and through the leaves now framing
the windshield
I could see the front of the car
disappearing into foliage.
Everywhere around me in the vehicle
plastic and metal
were becoming earth; the empty seat beside me
was now a flower bed
with roses and rhododendrons
about to open.
But the car's ride
began to be rough
and I poked my head through the laurel hedge
growing up the outside of the door
and saw the tires were no longer rubber
but looked more like tree trunks
forming around the spinning axles.
Thus, as I pulled into Vernon
the motor by this time halting and uneven too
I only just managed to locate John Lent's house
and turn up his driveway
where at the foot of his great green lawn
the entire construction that had been an automobile
stopped, and the sides
fell away like a cracked flowerpot
so I was left sitting
in a pleasant arbor
the stem of a young tree in my hand
and here were John and Jude coming smiling down the lawn
and all I could say
by way of explanation
was:
I'm home.

RAISING A RELATIONSHIP

It starts as two people enjoying themselves.
Months later, one of them gets a bit moody
and the other asks: "What's wrong?"
"Nothing," the first replies
but the other insists: "That's not true."
Then the first says: "I wasn't certain to begin with
but now I am. I checked and
whether you like it or not
we're having a relationship."
A silence. The first again:
"Of course, if you don't want to
I can always get rid of it."
A longer silence. Then the other:
"No, it's just . . . rather unexpected. But,"
cheering up,
"if you think about it,
it's marvellous." The two embrace
and life continues almost as before.

Except slowly the responsibility involved
becomes evident. One of the pair
out for a night on the town
decides to cut the evening short
because the other is home alone with the relationship.
Arguments now must be settled
with a minimum of fuss
for the relationship's sake.
Purchases are made on this basis, too.
"Let's go to Hawaii in December.
That'll be good for the relationship."
Various people aren't seen as often
due to their negative influence on the relationship.

And should the couple separate
there's the problem of custody.
Often one wants to keep it
and tries to convince the other to show more interest
though they are living apart.
Or, neither wishes it around in their new lives

and their friends become concerned
at how breezily the two fend off questions
about what happened to it.
Sometimes both would like the relationship
but don't want to be with each other
—which leads to a lot of confusion
as they attempt to sort this out.
Such uncertainty can drag on
until the relationship grows up and leaves on its own
determined, after all these years,
to have some fun.

HAMMER

A hammer is rising. A hammer
thrown up at the end of the day by a carpenter
with blood on the handle where his blisters have been.
A hammer. It lifts as well on the wave of steam
pouring up from the pots of a kitchen—a tiny kitchen
of an apartment, and that of a restaurant
serving a hundred customers at once.

A great cry of tedium
erupting out of papers and fluorescent glass
carries the hammer higher. It goes up end over end
on a tune broadcast to a million people.
And it climbs
on the force of a man's arm alone
flung straight up from the sickness that is his life.
It rises out of the weight of a body falling.

Nothing can stop it. The hammer has risen for centuries
high as the eaves, over the town. In this age
it has climbed to the moon
but it does not cease rising everywhere each hour.
And no one can say what it will drive
if at last it comes down.

PAPER, SCISSORS, STONE

An executive's salary for working with paper
beats the wage in a metal shop operating shears
which beats what a gardener earns arranging stone.

But the pay for a surgeon's use of scissors
is larger than that of a heavy equipment driver removing stone
which in turn beats a secretary's cheque for handling paper.

And, a geologist's hours with stone
nets more than a teacher's with paper
and definitely beats someone's time in a garment factory with
    scissors.

In addition: to manufacture paper,
you need stone to extract metal to fabricate scissors
to cut the product to size.
To make scissors you must have paper to write out the specs
and a whetstone to sharpen the new edges.
Creating gravel, you require the scissor-blades of the crusher
and lots of order forms and invoices at the office.

Thus I believe there is a connection
between things
and not at all like the hierarchy of winners
of a child's game.
When a man starts insisting
he should be paid more than me
because he's more important to the task at hand,
I keep seeing how the whole process collapses
if almost any one of us is missing.
When a woman claims she deserves more money
because she went to school longer,
I remember the taxes I paid to support her education.
Should she benefit twice?
Then there's the guy who demands extra
because he has so much seniority
and understands his work so well
he has ceased to care, does as little as possible,
or refuses to master the latest techniques

the new-hires are required to know.
Even if he's helpful and somehow still curious
after his many years—
again, nobody does the job alone.

Without a machine to precisely measure
how much sweat we each provide
or a contraption hooked up to electrodes in the brain
to record the amount we think,
my getting less than him
and more than her
makes no sense to me.
Surely whatever we do at the job
for our eight hours—as long as it contributes—
has to be worth the same.

And if anyone mentions
this is a nice idea but isn't possible,
consider what we have now:
everybody dissatisfied, continually grumbling and disputing.
No, I'm afraid it's the wage system that doesn't funcion
except it goes on
and will
until we set to work to stop it

with paper, with scissors, and with stone.

COUNTRY FEUDS

Out of town, disagreements between neighbors
are as simple as water:
water rights, diversion of creeks,
water lines
or shared wells that go dry. The feuds
grow naturally as animals:
grazing someone's cows
in return for a spring calf
or whether a quarter of a hog
is equal to a quarter of a heifer
in the fall. Some arguments
root deep in the purpose
of the country: people who want to operate
a small sawmill on their acreage
and the folks across the lane who moved here
for the quiet.

        Each winter
the troubles become more intense.
Somebody stops speaking to certain friends
whenever they meet in the village
and much later a phone call is made
Hey, are we having a quarrel?
If so, we can really get behind it.
And if not, don't be so surly when we see you.
These winter hassles are not limited
to a few miles of road. Strange letters to officials
—local, regional and national—
get written in the early darkness
on country tables
and mailed.

        At any season
you must be careful what you say.
Tree farm licences,
road access, ducks' eggs
versus chickens',
when carrots are tastiest and should be picked
—all can be tests. In each home

is a list, continually updated,
of which acquaintances are assets
and which liabilities, what stands on specific issues
are to be condemned.
An outsider or newcomer is allowed a few mistakes
but visitors who persistently express wrong opinions
or inquire too often after a name
currently not mentioned on this property
are subject to classification themselves.

To avoid these disputes
you have to stay in the city. Once you turn off the highway
onto dirt roads
you are headed
for a fight.

STUDENTS

The freshman class-list printouts
showed birthdates so recent
Wayman was sure the computer was in error.
One young man, however, was curious
about Wayman's mention near the start of term
of his old college newspaper:
"You were an editor *when*? Wow,
that's before I was born."

The wisdom of the students
hadn't altered, though.
Wayman observed many clung to
The Vaccination Theory of Education
he remembered: once you have had a subject
you are immune
and never have to consider it again.
Other students continued to endorse
The Dipstick Theory of Education:
as with a car engine, where as long as the oil level
is above the add line
there is no need to put in more oil,
so if you receive a pass or higher
why put any more into learning?

At the front of the room, Wayman sweated
to reveal his alternative.
"Adopt The Kung Fu Theory of Education,"
he begged.
"Learning as self-defence. The more you understand
about what's occurring around you
the better prepared you are to deal with difficulties."

The students remained skeptical.
A young woman was a pioneer
of The Easy Listening Theory of Learning:
spending her hours in class
with her tape recorder earphones on,
silently enjoying a pleasanter world.
"Don't worry, I can hear you,"

she reassured Wayman
when after some days he was moved to inquire.

Finally, at term's end
Wayman inscribed after each now-familiar name on the list
the traditional single letter.
And whatever pedagogical approach
he or the students espoused,
Wayman knew this notion would be pored over
with more intensity
than anything else Wayman taught.

from
**IN A SMALL HOUSE
ON THE OUTSKIRTS OF HEAVEN**
(1989)

ONE LUMP OR TWO

In your sugar bowl, *Frank said,*
sugar gets hard and sticks to the sides.
It's no different in the various silos
at the Spreckels mill.
Three of us are lowered on ropes
into a silo each shift,
dressed in a sort of moon suit
with pickaxe and shovel.
For the next eight
we pry the sugar from the walls.

Each time when I touched bottom
I'd say to myself: "It's a small step
for a man, but a giant leap
for the working class." The foreman
never went down. He's supposed to stay on top
to watch our ropes
but he regularly takes off somewhere.
Anyway, nobody bothers to be hauled up
when we have to take a piss.
We just let fly where we stand.
I stopped using sugar much when I got that work.

They had us on rotating shifts
which I didn't like.
But graveyards were best.
I or somebody would carve a bed
in the sugar, out of the foreman's line of vision.
We'd usually manage
to each grab a few hours sleep during the night.

Strangest part of the job, though,
was my boots. No mattter how clean they looked
when I took them off
or where in the house I left them
they'd both be completely covered with ants
when I'd go to put them on for work again.

THE BIG THEFT

for Howard White

It's one of those myths
from the workplace, told by somebody who is sure
the story is true. So you believe it, until

you find yourself listening to another version
of the tale. In this case
let's call it The Big Theft. I first heard it
in a truck assembly plant:

before you came, Tom, there was a guy,
Roger Hutchison, worked here:
an oldtimer. The guard caught him
at the gate one afternoon
leaving with an oil pressure gauge in his lunchkit.
Hell, we all take something home
if we can use it—clips or seat cushions—
Roger was just unlucky and got nabbed.
But for some reason they went around to his house
and discovered a nearly completed truck
in his garage. Over the years, he had boosted
piece by piece almost everything for it.
He'd obviously gotten help moving the larger items
like the frame or the engine
from the parts yard. But he had built
pretty damn close to an entire tractor unit
in his spare time.

Then at coffee
on a renovation job:
Donny used to be employed at a brickworks
where a man each day
took a brick home in his lunchbox.
Only one brick. But when the man dropped dead of a heart
    attack
the week before he was due to retire
they found he had stockpiled
a few bricks less than the total he needed
to construct his dream house.

How this myth began isn't hard to grasp.
Even the dullest among us can understand
no amount of money the company pays
really compensates for the time and effort
the job takes out of our lives.
As the slogan says: *the things we give up*
to go to work
are never returned. It's pleasant to imagine
some person someplace turning the tables.

And as with every myth, there's a lesson here.
This teaches we can gain possession
of what we make where we are employed
but not by acting alone.

Plus it is evident
rent-a-cops aren't posted at the office door at quitting time
to check the executives' briefcases
or certain envelopes addressed to the owners.
If these containers were opened
inside would be revealed
part of the value of the labor we perform each shift
being snuck out past the fence.
What these people remove secretly
isn't material required on the job
so they don't consider their actions stealing.
Yet from our work
a group of men and women get richer than us
without even asking us to vote
on whether we consent to this situation.
And that's
no myth.

HATING JEWS

How much work
it must be to despise the Jews.
Fourteen million people, or more:
a majority of whom you've never met
but every one
has to be hated. Anti-Semites surely deserve some credit
for undertaking this colossal task.

And speaking of Semites, what about women and men
who hate Arabs? There are more Arabs
than Jews: some who dwell in the desert
and can't read or write,
some who ride around in air-conditioned limousines
rich as Jews are supposed to be.
What an effort is required
to detest so many social groups:
urban, nomads, electronic
specialists, nurses, irrigation technicians.

Meantime, certain individuals
loathe Orientals. I think these haters
should receive an international prize
for their willingness to abhor such a high percentage
of their own species. But others
hate homosexuals
or lesbians, or all men
or women—the latter two projects
being probably the largest ever initiated
in human history.

Yet having an aversion
only to Jews
is such a mammoth endeavor
no wonder those who tackle it
look drained: faces twisted, body slumped.
A few pros after years of training
carry it off more comfortably.
But ordinary women and men who sign up for this activity
seem to my eyes heavily burdened.

And me? I am repulsed
by those human beings who do me harm.
I'm not as ambitious as
the big-league despisers, though.
I attempt to focus my disgust
on specific individuals
causing pain to myself or my friends.
It's true I've learned to dislike
some general classifications of people
—for example, landlords and employers.
But rather than loathe each one of them
I try to remember the source of their odiousness
is the structure that gives them
their power over me
and aim my rage at that.

So I'm not against hate. I consider some of it
excellent for the circulation: enough injustice
remains on this planet
to justify hate being with us a while yet.
My intent is
to see it directed
where it will do the most good.

THE POET MILTON ACORN CROSSES INTO THE
REPUBLIC OF HEAVEN

Somewhere west of his death, he stood
before a tall cottonwood or alder.
As on an autumn afternoon, the leaves
had turned to luminous yellows, shaking
in a wind, the motions of blades and stems
at times swaying to a unified falling and lifting
then back into hundreds of different flurries.

The walls of a bluff or canyon
rose behind the tree. And he saw
high in the branches
or the air, an energy
made visible, a cloud
drifting toward him.
When it touched ground, it took the form
almost of a person
blurred by a light emanating from itself
although appearing to be dressed in a white gown
with waist-length wings.

He was determined not to be awed
by anything metaphysical.
His hand reached for the shirt pocket
where he usually kept his cigars. Nothing.
"You're an angel?" he asked, gruffly as he could.
Despite himself, his voice sounded nervous
to his ears. *No.* The sweet accent
was neither male nor female.
This is a shape meant to be familiar to your species.

His hand shook slightly
as he patted his other shirt pocket.
Empty. He cleared his throat.
"As a dialectical materialist," he said,
"I have to tell you
your wings are too short.
I read once for a human-size body to stay airborne
its wings would need to be pretty damn large."

The figure in front of him shimmered.
While he strained to focus, the figure's wings
extended to reach the dusty soil.

"Much better," he said, attempting to keep the initiative.
"You wouldn't have a cigar on you?"
No response. He shrugged.
"Well, if you aren't an angel, are you a saint?
St. Peter, perhaps? Ready to judge if I'm worthy to pass
the Pearly Gates?" He jabbed out a finger.
"I never believed in
any afterlife. I used to say I wouldn't want to spend eternity
with any of the pious frauds and criminals
they're always telling us on Earth
get to go to Paradise."

There is only one life, the figure said.

"Then how is it I'm speaking with you?"
he replied. A cold gust shook the leaves.
The poet shivered.

Do you feel you merit an everlasting existence?
The figure's voice was curious.

"If I had to, I could testify to God himself
—or herself, come to think of it—
I was honest,
true to my class, my country, my art.
I was a good carpenter,
a builder first with wood, then words.
I spoke out for what I believe.
I shouted, 'Love!'"

Some days your mind fogged,
the figure said gently.
*It wasn't your fault. But evil and good,
master and victim
became confused for you toward the end. You roared
at the helpless as well as the guilty.*

Then he remembered
events he could not know before
and he felt ashamed.
After some moments, he muttered:
"I worked with what I had, didn't I?"

It's unimportant now, the figure said.
*Those things occurred in history. Here
you are out of time.
Soon you will abandon
the personality you grew, forever.*

A gust sent some of the intense yellow leaves
spiralling from the branches.

"Then why this talk?" he asked, bitterly.
"I thought when I died I would just disappear.
This is cruel: to bring me back
for a stupid chat. To have to die again.
I was disappointed by much when I was alive.
I never dreamed I would be disappointed by death."

It's cruel to be born, the figure said.

"Don't give me crap!" he replied.
Then, calmer,
"If it's going to end for me now,
actions speak louder than words.
Let me see God."

What? The figure sounded astonished.

"Yeah, if there really is one.
I want to make sense
of what happened, of meeting you.
That would make more of this fit together."

If you want to see God, you can,
the figure said.
And where the figure had been

a shape contracted
and swirled away, as if smoke,

so the poet saw the great tree
with the wind
like all the winds of the world
stirring the golden leaves.
Then stillness in the branches.
Then a wind again.

That is God, the voice of the figure said
from the air.

And as the poet watched the tree breathe,
he entered
the republic of the dark.

DEFECTIVE PARTS OF SPEECH:
HAVE YOU REALLY READ ALL THESE?

A wall of books in my house: a giant page of words
made from multicolored letters
formidable

       to some
who have learned instead or
also to read
water, for example
in the bay
with a southeast wind
how the currents and fish respond

or the park warden looking at sign
See? The coyote have been eating the deer.

Ernie Frank stopping where the trail has exposed
soil horizons, showing us
what they reveal

Or the mountain guide explaining
how he interprets snow: the amount the crystals tell
by their shape and dampness

You think we didn't have clocks?
the elder asked Sandy Cameron
*The tide was our clock. We understood
the time of day and day of the year
from the tide.*

And the people who decipher accurately
the face of those they love
or hate

My insurance agent who insists
*I know who is most likely to have a car accident
by how they walk into this office.*

Men and women who study
the world
picking up warnings and
diagnoses, remedies
and fables

—all these
and more

MARSHALL-WELLS ILLUMINATION

for Jim Daniels

One bright morning, I was sent
to the wholesale cash-and-carry hardware,
glad to be out of the pounding and saws
of the jobsite, to drive the city streets
and walk into the wooden-floored building.

At the counter, the lone clerk
I had spoken with several times before
—an old man, surely past retirement—
fussed at his order books, precise
as his usual shirt and tie
concerning *common* or *finishing*
galvanized or *not*,
lengths and amounts needed.
The stock numbers were passed
to somebody else for fulfillment
and I stood waiting, in my workclothes and boots.
Motes of dust
rose and drifted in the sunlight
that leaned in from windows down the long room
where a dozen other people toiled at desks.
Then a man entered
from outside, older than me,
younger than the clerk, dressed in coveralls
and leather carpenter's apron.
He pulled a list from a pocket
and stepped aside, as the counter clerk
bent once more to flip the pages of the catalogs
to set the number of each item
on the proper form.

And the man in coveralls
perhaps for pleasure at the new day,
suddenly shifted his heavy boots back and forth
in a clumsy part of a dance
and stopped, grinning.

The motion caught the clerk's eye, and he frowned.
But the man
stomped his boots
in another quick pattern. He paused
under the clerk's dour gaze,
then resumed: the thick soles toeing the planks
and tipping back on heels,
nails falling from the pouches of his apron
as his arms flew out for balance. The man,
laughing, looked over at me for approval.
And the clerk also faced in my direction
shaking his head to invite me to mock
the ridiculous swaying.

                         But at this moment
       I knew
neither gravity nor
centrifigal force
spins the Earth through space.
Our planet revolves
under the dancing feet of this man
and those like him: through their efforts
the immense bulk of our home
is moved. And I understood
as the boots crashed down, this joy
finds even in the dreadful agreements we labor in
the love required to trample
what we have been given
under our invincible shoes.

                         Yet the three of us
hung suspended
in the amber light:
Grandfather Paper and Order,
Father Happiness and Measuring Tape
and myself. The rest of the office watched us
from their file drawers and typewriters
as I saw the planet lurch forward
with each kick of these feet
and the earth also pushed on
by the weight of an invoice

dropped from an aged hand, saw Father and Grandfather
both turned
to ask me to choose
—one motionless, the other beginning to slow.

What could I do
but dance?

NEW POEMS

DID I MISS ANYTHING?

*Question frequently asked by
students after missing a class*

Nothing. When we realized you weren't here
we sat with our hands folded on our desks
in silence, for the full two hours

> Everything. I gave an exam worth
> 40 per cent of the grade for this term
> and assigned some reading due today
> on which I'm about to hand out a quiz
> worth 50 per cent

Nothing. None of the content of this course
has value or meaning
Take as many days off as you like:
any activities we undertake as a class
I assure you will not matter either to you or me
and are without purpose

> Everything. A few minutes after we began last time
> a shaft of light descended and an angel
> or other heavenly being appeared
> and revealed to us what each woman or man must do
> to attain divine wisdom in this life and
> the hereafter
> This is the last time the class will meet
> before we disperse to bring this good news to all people
> on earth

Nothing. When you are not present
how could something significant occur?

> Everything. Contained in this classroom
> is a microcosm of human existence
> assembled for you to query and examine and ponder
> This is not the only place such an opportunity has been
> gathered

but it was one place

And you weren't here

BILLY ON INDUSTRIAL PROGRESS

He's down in the big garden
on a cold day
early November
before the snow
having left the autumn rototilling
this late, and Joan's old machine
can't really handle
the frozen topsoil
or maybe the icy temperature
but in any case
the engine dies every few meters
and when it does start again
the machine spurts ahead as the tines
suddenly climb on top
of the hard ground
and race across the surface
snapping Billy's head back
as he's yanked after
until he gets the device
settled in again
and turned to cover the part of the row
it missed

At the moment, though
the rototiller is on its side in the dirt
having stalled out once more
and Billy is looking at it
like he'd kick it
except he knows he would kick it so hard
he'd break his foot
and that would hurt
too
so instead he stands in the field yelling
to inform the crows and jays
nothing has gone right for the human race
since the industrial revolution
and the Luddites were right
wanting to smash all machinery
and there are people in this Valley

he knows, personally
who will tell you the wheel
was invented by a woman
and since the wheel is the basis
for every machine ever invented
it isn't hard to point the finger
at just who is responsible
for things being
the way they are

POETRY OVERDOSE

Each day on the planet Earth
a million poems are written
Of these, English-speaking North America
accounts for roughly ten per cent:
a hundred thousand poems
In a year, then
more than thirty-six million
appear on this continent
on lined paper, notebook pages
and computer printouts
I have no proof
these numbers are correct
but they sound right to me
And, as any poet knows, if something sounds good
it must be true

Of the thirty-six million poems produced here annually
maybe one day's worth succeed in being published
—in a plum, mass circulation magazine
or in the fifty copies of the first and last issue
of a photocopied venture
intended to save the art form from being marginalized
Perhaps ten thousand of these printed poems
appear again in their authors' books
during the following three years:
whether volumes issued by a nationally-distributed press
or a collection the poet pays for herself or himself
tries to sell at local readings
and eventually gives away
About a thousand of the poems in books
get chosen over the next five years
for anthologies
—thematic, ethnic, geographic
And at the end of ten years
of these thousand anthologized poems
only sixteen
are still being reprinted
although during this interval a few thousand others

have flashed an additional time and died
in a handful of poets' selected poems

From more than thirty-six million
to sixteen
in a decade
is such a rate of attrition
no wonder we never stop
jotting down phrases
jabbing at keyboards

With poems, as with mosquitoes
millions must be born each breeding season
so a pitifully small percentage
can annoy you when you try to sleep
give you satisfaction when you smack them down
draw blood